Frank O'Hara
and the Poetics of Saying "I"

Frank O'Hara and the Poetics of Saying "I"

Micah Mattix

Madison • Teaneck
Fairleigh Dickinson University Press

Published by Fairleigh Dickinson University Press
Co-published with The Rowman & Littlefield Publishing Group, Inc.
4501 Forbes Boulevard, Suite 200, Lanham, Maryland 20706
www.rlpgbooks.com

Estover Road, Plymouth PL6 7PY, United Kingdom

British Library Cataloguing in Publication Information Available

Library of Congress Cataloging-in-Publication Data

Library of Congress Cataloguing-in-Publication Data on file under LC#2010024715
ISBN: 978-1-61147-046-8 (cl. : alk. paper)
eISBN: 978-1-61147-047-5

∞ ™The paper used in this publication meets the minimum requirements of American National Standard for Information Sciences—Permanence of Paper for Printed Library Materials, ANSI/NISO Z39.48-1992.

Printed in the United States of America

CONTENTS

Acknowledgments

I WOULD LIKE TO THANK A NUMBER OF PEOPLE AND ORGANIZATIONS without whom I would have never completed this work. I received much-needed financial support from the Swiss National Science Foundation for a research year at Yale. Melissa Watterwork of the Thomas J. Dodd Research Center at the University of Connecticut assisted me with O'Hara's unpublished letters, and I am indebted to the staff at both the Beinecke Rare Book and Manuscript Library at Yale and the Rare Book Collection at the Wilson Library at the University of North Carolina, Chapel Hill for their help with rare versions of O'Hara's art criticism. I would also like to thank Elsa Dorfman, who answered a number of questions regarding O'Hara's involvement with Paterson Society.

Peter Halter was kind enough to read a number of earlier versions of the entire work and each time offered gracious, cogent advice that helped me to expand the original thesis in fruitful directions. Patrick Vincent, Lukas Erne, and Thomas Austenfeld have assisted me in various ways in this project, and I would like to thank them here for their respective encouragement and support. I have benefited greatly from the guidance of the late Robert Rehder, who read a number of earlier versions of the manuscript and offered numerous suggestions and helped me understand what it means to be a true scholar of poetry. I would also like to thank Christine Retz and Joshua Allen for their guidance in bringing the manuscript to press and Wyatt Benner for his expert copyediting.

Anne-Claude and Nicolas Suter, Terry and Diana Mattix, and Roger and Mary-Claude Moret supported me in my research in numerous ways, and I would like to thank them here for their assistance. While thanks extended to one's spouse are staples of acknowledgment sections, it is nevertheless true that I could not have completed this work without Carine's patience and support over the years, and I would like to acknowledge that it is as much the result of her gracious sacrifices as it is of my research.

For permission to include the material below, I would like to thank the following:

Alfred A. Knopf, a division of Random House, Inc., for permission to quote from *The Collected Poems of Frank O'Hara* by Frank O'Hara, edited by Donald Allen, copyright © 1971 by Maureen Granville-Smith, Administratix of the Estate of Frank O'Hara, copyright renewed 1999 by Maureen O'Hara Granville-Smith, and Donald Allen Introduction copyright © 1971 by Alfred A. Knopf.

City Lights Books, for permission to quote from *Lunch Poems*, copyright © 1964 by Frank O'Hara.

Grove/Atlantic, Inc., for permission to quote from *Meditations in an Emergency*, copyright © 1957 by Frank O'Hara.

A version of chapter 3 originally appeared in *American Poetry: Whitman to the Present*, ed. Robert Rehder and Patrick Vincent (Tübingen: Gunter Narr Verlag, 2006), 139–149. I would like to thank the publisher for permission to reprint it here.

Abbreviations

AC	*Art Chronicles, 1954–1966.* By Frank O'Hara. New York: George Braziller, 1975.
CP	*The Collected Poems of Frank O'Hara.* Ed. Donald Allen. 2nd ed. Berkeley and Los Angeles: University of California Press, 1995.
EW	*Early Writing.* By Frank O'Hara. Ed. Donald Allen. Bolinas, CA: Grey Fox, 1977.
FOH	*Frank O'Hara: Poet among Painters.* By Marjorie Perloff. 2nd ed. Chicago: University of Chicago Press, 1998.
SS	*Standing Still and Walking in New York.* By Frank O'Hara. Ed. Donald Allen. San Francisco: Grey Fox, 1975.

Frank O'Hara and the Poetics of Saying "I"

Introduction: Frank O'Hara and His Critics; The Case of Marjorie Perloff

THE POETRY OF FRANK O'HARA (1926–66) IS DIFFERENT FROM THAT OF many of his contemporaries. Some forty years after his death, however, his work is still largely misunderstood. As Marjorie Perloff points out, in the years that directly followed his fatal accident on Fire Island, New York, O'Hara's poetry was often dismissed as the work of an idiosyncratic minor poet, written at a specific time and place for a limited audience, and, therefore, worthy of little interest (*FOH*, xi–xii). Perloff notes that in 1966, for example, Gilbert Sorrentino writes that *Lunch Poems* (1964) is part of "a world of wry elegance, of gesture, a world made up of a certain kind of strictly New York joie de vivre."[1] In 1971, Herbert Leibowitz, in his review of *The Collected Poems of Frank O'Hara* (1971), writes that O'Hara was a "fascinating amalgam of fan, connoisseur, and propagandist," a man who was "the Apollinaire of his generation, an aesthetic courtier who had taste and impudence and prodigious energy." His poetry, he says, exhibits "a precocious air of command and a throwaway charm."[2] In 1978, Thomas Byrom writes that the poems collected in the posthumous *Early Writing* (1977) and *Poems Retrieved* (1977) "are from a catalogue of late Victorian camp, a matter of excellent personal taste."[3] In each of these reviews, while O'Hara is praised for his distinctive style, his distinctiveness is characterized in terms of "Victorian camp" and "strictly New York joie de vivre"—terms that make the implicit claim that his work is less important than the work of his contemporaries.

In 1972, however, while preparing a review essay on the volumes of poetry published in the preceding two years, Perloff herself read Ron Padgett and David Shapiro's *Anthology of New York Poets* (1970), in which O'Hara's poetry figured prominently. After having read O'Hara's work, Perloff too felt that his poetry was different. Unlike Sorrentino, Leibowitz, and Byrom, however, she became convinced as she read his work that he should be considered "one of the central poets" of the so-called postwar period (*FOH*, xxxii). "The more

O'Hara I read," she would later recall, "the more enthusiastic I became about his work" (xxxi–xxxii). "Here was a writer who made poetry look like a delightful game but who also had an uncanny way of getting what John Ashbery has called, with reference to Picabia, 'the perishable fragrance of tradition' into his work" (xxxii). "The age," Perloff continues, needed "a *raison d'être* for O'Hara's casual, improvisatory, nonmetrical and generally nonstanzaic 'I do this, I do that' pieces, pieces that hardly seemed to qualify as *poems* at all" (xiii). Hence her *Frank O'Hara: Poet among Painters* (1978), in which she argues that O'Hara is a "serious" poet, indebted in particular to painters such as Jackson Pollock (1912–56) and French poets such as Arthur Rimbaud (1854–91) and Guillaume Apollinaire (1880–1918).

For Perloff, the source of O'Hara's original style is his break from the symbolist tradition in poetry. He writes using a version of surrealist automatism, where he expresses the coming into being of conscious experience in language that lacks rational coherence. In this sense, O'Hara does not use words, Perloff claims, as signs to represent his feelings; rather, he fuses his feelings with the material elements of the words and structure of his poems. For Perloff, what holds his poems together as wholes is not predetermined themes or formal structures but rather the "tension" of the "surface" of the completed works, which is said, in turn, to be akin to the "surface" of Pollock's abstract paintings (*FOH*, 23). O'Hara's poems, Perloff claims, create irreducible semantic ambiguities, which, in turn, are "equivalent to the painter's 'push and pull'—the spatial tensions that keep a surface alive and moving"—and thus make for poems that have no "beginning, middle, and end" and that are of "great speed, openness, flexibility, and defiance of expectations" (131, 135).

Perloff's book is both rich and insightful, and provides a helpful introduction to O'Hara's work. She is correct, for example, to note O'Hara's expressionist poetics and the value he himself placed on the process of artistic creation. There is no doubt, furthermore, that O'Hara was indebted to the example of Rimbaud and the work of Pollock, and that his use of proper names and parataxis is at the heart of what makes his work so different. However, as helpful as Perloff's book is, there are two problems with it. First, she overstates O'Hara's debt to painting. O'Hara's interaction with painters in New York City from the early 1950s to the mid-1960s confirmed rather than created his views regarding artistic creation—views that were established through his interest in all the arts, including the music of Sergei Rachmaninoff (1873–1943) and John Cage (1912–92) and the poetry of

Walt Whitman (1818–92), Rainer Maria Rilke (1875–1926), William Carlos Williams (1883–1963), and Boris Pasternak (1890–1960), among others. Second, her more detailed readings of O'Hara's work sometimes lack precision—in particular her reading of the "surface" of O'Hara's poems—because in her use of the language of art criticism to discuss the formal elements of his poems she provides too little explanation as to what these terms might mean in relation to writing. Perloff's use of such language might be expected from a book first published by George Braziller, the famed arts and foreign literature publishing house in New York, and from a book with the subtitle "Poet among Painters," thus evoking Francis Steegmuller's well-known *Apollinaire, Poet among the Painters* (1963). The reason she uses such terms, as she makes clear in one of her first published pieces on O'Hara, is that she believes that the traditional vocabulary of poetry criticism is inadequate for discussing O'Hara's highly idiosyncratic work.[4] Yet, Perloff's use of painting terms such as "frottage," "push-pull," "surface," "depth," and "catalogue raisonné" is limiting in its own right, as we shall see in a moment (*FOH*, 42, 82–3).

Perloff's rightly motivated but sometimes too facile application of such terms to O'Hara's work, has been repeated by a number of critics since 1978, and now it is not uncommon to read critics who seem to begin with the assumption that the formal aspects of O'Hara's poems differ from those in Pollock's paintings in no significant way. This is not to say that there have not been some very helpful studies on O'Hara's relationship to painting since Perloff. In his chapter on O'Hara in *Savage Sight, Constructed Noise: Poetic Adaptations of Painterly Techniques in the French and American Avant-Gardes* (2003), David LeHardy Sweet, for example, provides an excellent, nuanced evaluation of how O'Hara's work is similar to Pollock's and other painters' work, such as that of Willem de Kooning (1904–97) and Larry Rivers (1923–2002). Yet, how it is different, while noted, is not examined in detail. While Sweet admits that O'Hara himself maintained a "categorical distinction between the arts," he too quickly dismisses this by arguing that O'Hara arrived at this distinction as a result of his search for "residues of communication" and "symptoms of filiation" between them.[5] This dismissal is, in part, due to the focus of Sweet's book, but it does not do justice to the difference between O'Hara's work and that of the so-called abstract expressionists.

Interestingly enough, Perloff's book has been one of the main catalysts for another approach to O'Hara's work. For a growing number of critics who have applied the theories of poststructuralism to O'Hara's poetry,[6] her conclusion that O'Hara expresses his feelings in the "push-pull" tension of the "surface" of his poems has proven to be an important starting point, along with Charles Altieri's 1973 article for the *Iowa Review* comparing O'Hara's compositional practices to Jacques Derrida's notion of "différence." The crowning example of this approach is Hazel Smith's *Hyperscapes in the Poetry of Frank O'Hara: Difference/Homosexuality/Topography* (2000). For Smith, what most distinguishes O'Hara is his use of "hyperscapes"—a term that she has coined to refer to various types of difference in his work, including textual, spatial, sexual, and political.[7] In her definition of the "textual difference" of O'Hara's work, Smith cites Perloff's argument concerning the "surface" of O'Hara's poems. Perloff, Smith argues, rightly shows how O'Hara "destabilizes the meaning" of his poems and creates "an overlaying of different meanings" in his use of indeterminate language.[8] She then, in effect, restates Perloff's argument in Derridean terms. It is perhaps no surprise, then, that while for Perloff O'Hara is a "poet among painters," for Smith he is "the arch-deconstructionist."[9]

It needs to be noted that a great number of O'Hara's poems do indeed lack formal coherence. O'Hara's poems also often simultaneously possess more than one meaning because of his use of indeterminate or ambiguous phrases, parataxis, or proper nouns and simple verbs that lack rich connotative meaning, and Perloff's and Smith's understanding of his use of language can be applied—with a few important modifications—to poems such as *Second Avenue*. This lack of formal coherence is related, in part, to O'Hara's understanding of art as a form of expression, where the poet is said to express his feelings in the material of the creative medium rather than to represent some predetermined object or image. This is a notion that O'Hara gleaned from expressionist painters, as well as from poets such as Rilke and Pasternak. However, while O'Hara understood creation to be a form of expression, he did not hold that the mechanics of expression in poetry were no different from the mechanics of expression in painting. Words have a de facto representational element—this is what makes them words—and O'Hara recognized this. Furthermore, while there are some similarities between O'Hara's work and the theories of poststructuralists such as Derrida, it is reductive to treat O'Hara as a mere forerunner of Derridean deconstruction. While his poems are sometimes disconnected and lack an explicit thematic coherence, this does not mean that he somehow avoids using language as language or that his poems contain no themes other than that of "destabilizing" meaning.

One of the difficult things about O'Hara's work is his refusal to be pigeonholed. Regarding Larry Rivers, who most resembles O'Hara in his antitheoretical position with respect to artistic creation, O'Hara once wrote: "He shifts and feints like Sugar Ray Robinson, if you double he redoubles like George Rapée. He is an enigma, and he is fascinating" (*SS*, 97). Indeed, so is O'Hara in some respects. It could be said that the sole constant in O'Hara's work is its lack of consistent theoretical or aesthetic convictions; however, this too would be an overstatement. Nevertheless, there is needed a fuller, less reductive account of O'Hara's work that is flexible enough to take into consideration his stylistically diverse work. The present work is an effort to provide such an account.

While still acknowledging O'Hara's debt to the so-called abstract expressionists, this work will place O'Hara's work in the context of poets such as Rilke, Williams and Pasternak, among others, and show how O'Hara differed from these artists with respect to his mechanics and the value he attributed to the completed work. While O'Hara, like Pollock and Pasternak, understands art to be an expression of feeling (which, in turn, is understood to be analogous to the energy or power at work in the material world), the end of art, for O'Hara, is not so much to tell us about these elemental forces that shape the material world, but rather to renew our experience of it. This does not mean that art does not tell us something about our feelings and about the world in which we live. However, for O'Hara, it does not express, in André Breton's (1896–1966) words, some hitherto imperceptible "superior reality," or detail some "supreme language," as Stéphane Mallarmé (1842–98) hoped.[10] It is this somewhat less ambitious, more pragmatic view of art that, in the end, most distinguishes O'Hara's work from the work of previous poets and from the work of a number of his contemporaries. Before a new evaluation of O'Hara's work is offered, however, the claim that O'Hara somehow uses words in the way that Pollock uses paint, and the theory of language implicit in such a claim, must first be examined in detail.

"Why I Am Not a Painter"

While it is often claimed that O'Hara's use of language in his poems is similar to Pollock's use of paint in his abstract paintings, this notion fails to take into consideration the essential differences between the two mediums. Nowhere are these differences clearer than in O'Hara's poem "Why I Am Not a Painter" (1956). While the poem is light and humorous, O'Hara makes a serious distinction between painting and poetry. Indeed, O'Hara often uses humor when referring to his own work or aesthetics simply to keep from sounding too self-important.

In the poem, O'Hara compares the processes of creation in Mike Golderg's painting *Sardines* (1955) and his own poem "Oranges: 12 Pastorals" (1949). While there are a number of similarities, in particular between the *process* of creation in painting and the *process* of creation in writing, O'Hara also makes a number of distinctions. In fact, the title of the poem is a play on a proposed but never completed book by Apollinaire called *Et moi aussi je suis peintre* (*And I Too Am a Painter*), the advertisement of which was printed at the end of Robert Motherwell's 1949 translation of Apollinaire's *Les peintres cubistes* (1913). In his chapter on Picasso, Apollinaire writes that Picasso uses words and numbers in his paintings as "pictorial elements."[11] While Apollinaire did not argue that a poet could use words as paint, as is clear from his *Calligrammes* (1918), he tried to apply the cubist notion of simultaneism and bring the "plastic" elements of words to the fore.[12] In his poem, however, O'Hara highlights the material differences between poetry and paint.

The opening lines of the poem state that it will be about "why" O'Hara is not a painter—that is, "why" what O'Hara does cannot be considered painting. Despite this, O'Hara begins with a shared aspect of his and Goldberg's work: both are created out of a process of exploration. O'Hara writes:

WHY I AM NOT A PAINTER

I am not a painter, I am a poet.
Why? I think I would rather be
a painter, but I am not. Well,

for instance, Mike Goldberg
is starting a painting. I drop in.
"Sit down and have a drink" he
says. I drink; we drink. I look
up. "You have SARDINES in it."
"Yes, it needed something there."
"Oh." I go and the days go by
and I drop in again. The painting

is going on, and I go, and the days
go by. I drop in. The painting is
finished. "Where's SARDINES?"
All that's left is just
letters, "It was too much," Mike says.
But me? One day I am thinking of
a color: orange. I write a line
about orange. Pretty soon it is a
whole page of words, not lines.
Then another page. There should be
so much more, not of orange, of
words, of how terrible orange is
and life. Days go by. It is even in
prose, I am a real poet. My poem
is finished and I haven't mentioned
orange yet. It's twelve poems, I call
it ORANGES. And one day in a gallery
I see Mike's painting, called SARDINES.

(*CP*, 262)

O'Hara notes that Goldberg begins with the word "SARDINES," not because the painting is about sardines but because the painting "needed something." This nonchalant explanation of Goldberg's artistic decision implies that the word "SARDINES" is used for no other reason than that it happened to be available. O'Hara himself begins with "thinking of a color," which happens to be "orange." He begins with orange not because the poem will be about the color—after all, he finishes the poem and does not even mention the color—but because he happened to be thinking of orange. While the ironic inversion of Goldberg beginning with a word and O'Hara beginning with a color could be used to claim that O'Hara equates painting and poetry, the opposite is in fact the case, as we shall see in a moment. What is important here is that the word "SARDINES" and the color orange are the respective starting points for both Goldberg's and O'Hara's exploration of their feelings in the material of their mediums. Both artists produce, after a number of days, a completed work that does not contain the initial word or color. Goldberg's painting entitled SARDINES no longer has the word "SARDINES" in it (though it still contains some of the letters), and O'Hara's poem "ORANGES" does not contain the word "orange" in the completed text of what are now twelve poems.

Despite this shared aesthetic of exploration, there are a number of differences between the two works that are related to the differences between the two mediums. The first is found in how both Goldberg and O'Hara explore themselves in the materials of their respective mediums. While Goldberg both adds and suppresses images and words, O'Hara only adds words. Furthermore, this addition of words seems to be paratactical. The seeming speed of composition ("I write a line / about orange. Pretty soon it is a / whole page of words, not lines") and O'Hara's reference to his nascent poem as a "page of words" implies that what holds the poem together as a unit is the material limits of the page itself and not some unifying theme or subject matter to which all of the words on the page are related. While O'Hara could, of course, return to previous sections of the poem and delete words, the mechanics of writing itself means that such a return would be perceived as an act of editing and not as an act of exploration. Unlike Golderg's layering, deleting words in a poem neither seems spontaneous nor leaves a trace of the original word or phrase. While O'Hara could have used a line to strike through a particular word or phrase, which would leave a trace of the original word or phrases, such an action would seem too planned. O'Hara, of course, did revise his poems; however, it was important to him that his work appear spontaneous."I don't believe in reworking—*too much*," he writes tellingly (*SS*, 21, emphasis added).

This leads to a second difference between the two works, which is found in the respective scales of each. While Goldberg's exploration of paint takes place on a predetermined scale, O'Hara's exploration creates the scale of the work as he writes. This has important implications, as we shall see in a moment, for the use of painting terms such as "push-pull" and "surface," because these terms assume a predetermined scale.

A third difference between Goldberg's painting and O'Hara's poem is found in the nonrepresentational use of words. O'Hara points to the fact that while a painter can use words or letters as abstract expressive images, a poet must use them, at least in part, as representational vehicles for no other reason than that part of what makes a word a word is its representational function. For example, Goldberg uses the word "SARDINES" in his painting not because the painting is a representation of sardines or the word "SARDINES," but rather because in the process of exploring his feelings in his materials, Goldberg finds that it needs the image of the word "SARDINES" much in the same manner that it might need a bit of blue here or a bit of red there. The fact that he later discovers that the word "SARDINES" is "too much" underlines the use of the word as a nonfigurative expression of the painter's feelings. This abstract expression of the artist's feelings through letters in painting is quite different from the poet's expression of his feelings in words. While the poem is not about the color orange, the poet, unlike the painter, cannot express his feelings in pure abstraction, but must use words, which, in turn, evoke the concrete objects or concepts represented in them. Therefore, while O'Hara writes that his poem is not "of orange" but "of words," he immediately adds "of how terrible orange is / and life."

The notion that the poet cannot escape the de facto representational element of words is underscored in the poem in Goldberg's decision to begin with a word and O'Hara's decision to begin with a color. Because Goldberg is a painter, everything he uses in his paintings, even the word "SARDINES" is a "pictorial element." As a poet, however, O'Hara cannot use a word as a "pictorial element" alone, even if he can direct our attention to the material elements of words. Indeed, even pure "pictorial elements," such as color, must be represented with a word or a string of words. This is the reason that O'Hara distinguished, on at least two occasions, between painting and poetry in terms of "naming." In "Memorial Day 1950," for example, which will be discussed in detail in the following chapter, O'Hara writes that "naming things is only the intention / to make things," and in "To Larry Rivers" (1954), he writes: "You do what I can only name" (*CP*, 18, 128). In both of these remarks, O'Hara contrasts a poem's inescapable linguistic nature with the made things of painting and the plastic arts.

If this is the case, it is problematic to apply painting terms, as Perloff does, such as "surface" and "push-pull" to O'Hara's poems. As far as the term "surface" is concerned, for example Perloff seems to have two rather different definitions of it that slip in and out of the book depending on the needs of the argument. On the one hand, she uses "surface" to refer to the absence of symbolism, while, on the other, she uses it to refer to the absence of representational content. Nowhere is this double definition clearer than in a passage from her opening chapter where she defines the "surface" of O'Hara's poems with reference to the "surface" of Pollock's paintings. As Perloff points out, O'Hara referred to the surface of his own poems on two separate occasions. First, in his "Notes on *Second Avenue*" (1953), he writes that, "the verbal elements [of the poem] are not too interesting to discuss although they are intended consciously to keep the surface of the poem high and dry, not wet, reflective and self-conscious" (*CP*,

497). Second, in a 1957 letter to Larry Rivers, which Rivers incorporated into a collage, he writes: "Now please tell me if you think these poems are filled with disgusting self-pity, if there are 'holes' in them, if the surface isn't kept 'up,' if there are recognizable images, if they show nostalgia for the avant-garde, or they don't have 'push' and 'pull,' and I'll keep working on them until each is a foot high" (quoted in *FOH*, 22).

To define O'Hara's use of the term "surface" in these two instances, Perloff turns to O'Hara's monograph on Jackson Pollock (1959). In it, she points out that O'Hara defines the "surface" of Pollock's paintings as the "field" where "the physical energies of the artist operate in actual detail, in full scale" (*FOH*, 23). She then applies this definition of "surface" to O'Hara's poems:

> The *surface* of the painting, and by analogy the *surface* of the poem, must, then, be regarded as a field upon which the physical energies of the artist can operate, without mediation of metaphor or symbol. The poet's images—for example, the "hum-colored / cabs," the "yellow helmets" worn by the laborers, or the "glass of papaya juice" in "A Step Away From Them"—are not symbolic properties; there is nothing behind these surfaces. Rather, their positioning in the poet's field, their push and pull interaction, function metonymically to create a microcosm of the poet's New York world—a world verifiable on any city map yet also fictive in its fantastic configurations. (*FOH*, 23)

While Perloff uses the word "surface" in this passage to refer to "images" that lack symbolic significance, arguing in the subsequent paragraph that this "distrust of symbolism is a central tenet of O'Hara's poetic," she implies that the "images" also somehow lack representational content. This is implied in her statement that "there is nothing behind" the surface of the words of the poem, and that the "surface" of the poem is the "field" on which O'Hara's "physical energies" somehow "operate, without mediation of metaphor or symbol." That Perloff is using the word "symbol" here in its linguistic rather than literary sense is perhaps underscored when she claims that the words of his poems are not "symbolic properties," which seems to mean that they are not signs, rather than claiming, for example, that they lack symbolic *significance*, which would mean that the words of the poem, while representational, do not have some second or third meaning.[13]

While Perloff is correct to point to O'Hara's interest in the material nature of language, this interest cannot be discussed in the same terms that one discusses a painter's interest in the plasticity and color of paint, for the simple reason that words and paint are different kinds of stuff. In painting criticism, for example, the term "surface" is used to refer to the artist's use of the horizontal and the perpendicular dimensions of the canvas, and the term "depth" to refer to the illusion of a third dimension. In the cubist paintings of Pablo Picasso (1881–1973) and Georges Braque (1882–1963), however, the surface is not used as a means of providing the paintings with a more "accurate" re-creation of visual perception, but rather to create the illusion that the partial forms of the paintings are, in fact, protruding out of the canvas.[14]

When applied to the nonfigurative work of Jackson Pollock, the terms "surface" and "depth" still refer to the distinction between the two-dimensional plane of the canvas and the illusion of a third dimension. In Pollock, however, there is a difference, as there is in cubism, in how "depth" is created and in what it signifies. First, "depth" is no longer created through the interaction of two-dimensional images in Pollock's nonfigurative works in the way that it is in the relative size and position of figures with respect to a vanishing point in the canvas in Raphael Sanzio's *The School of Athens* (1509–11), or in the superimposition of spatial planes, as in cubism. Rather, it is created through the spatial relationship of points of color in the paint itself. This is Hans Hofmann's classic point, when he writes, for example, in "The Search for the Real in the Visual Arts" (1948) that "depth" in Pollock's paintings "in a pictorial plastic sense is not created by the arrangement of objects one after another toward a vanishing point, in the sense of Renaissance perspective, but on the contrary by the creation of forces in the sense of push and pull."[15] Drawing from Wassily Kandinsky's distinction in *Concerning the Spiritual in Art* (1911) between warm, advancing colors and cold, retreating ones, Hofmann defines push-pull as the use of cool colors (blues and greens) to pull the picture backward and the use of hot colors (reds and yellows) to push the picture forward.[16] Thus, depth becomes part of the material surface of the paint rather than an illusion, and is used, in turn, to express or evoke cognitive states or emotions rather than to re-create visual experience.

While it may be possible in painting to express one's feelings in the material "surface" of paint itself (to which "depth" has now been assimilated), the notion that one can do so with the material element of words alone does not hold up under close scrutiny. Thus, while David LeHardy Sweet suggests, following both Perloff and Smith, that poets such as O'Hara use fragmentation to join the "the signifier and its referent" at the "level of the sign itself as a material fact or facet," this ignores the fact that in Western languages, at least, the meaning of words cannot be fused with the typography of signs alone, even if O'Hara uses what he calls "verbal elements" to *highlight* the material elements of words, as we shall see in chapter 2.[17]

Furthermore, it misunderstands O'Hara's remarks on the "surface" of his poems in his "Notes on *Second Avenue*." After stating that he hopes that the meaning of the poem and the surface of the poem are one, O'Hara adds: "I hope the poem to *be* the subject, not just about it" (*CP*, 497). O'Hara's main point in his "Notes" is that the meaning of the poem cannot be reduced to its constituent parts, but is found at the level of the completed work itself. Far from saying anything radical in these notes, O'Hara is restating (albeit using the occasional painting term) the ideas of both Pasternak and Pound concerning form and poetic meaning.

Recalling Pasternak's remark that the work of art as a whole "does not lend itself to quotation," O'Hara claims that the meaning of his poem cannot be reduced to its constituent parts, and states somewhat begrudgingly: "These notes which I'm attaching to the excerpts sometimes indicate, because you requested it, a more detailed identification of the subject matter (in some cases just a last name) than I wanted in the poem itself because it is beside the poem's point in most cases; elsewhere the remarks are explanatory of what I now feel my *attitude* was toward the material, not explanatory of the meaning which I don't think can be paraphrased (or at least I hope it can't)" (*CP*, 495). The notion that the work of art cannot be paraphrased is common among artists, and has been in existence since at least Coluccio Salutati's *De laboribus Herculis* (1406), which argues that the discourse of poetry ("poeticum narrationem") is distinct from other forms of representation.[18] For O'Hara, however, *Second Avenue* cannot be paraphrased not so much because it is a different form of expression than prose (which, of course, it is), but because the meaning it embodies is not represented in the words alone but enacted in the verbal elements of the poem as well. Therefore, it cannot be reduced to a descriptive prose statement without losing something of its overall significance.

Perloff runs into a similar problem in her use of the phrase "push-pull," which she defines later in the book as the use of "syntactic and prosodic devices" to create a surface "energy" (*FOH*, 135). While Perloff does not analyze O'Hara's use of these devices in detail, she is correct to note that O'Hara uses them in his poems and that his use of them is related, in part, to his poetics of expression. However, it can be confusing to claim, as she does, that the "tension" or "energy" that these devices create is "equivalent" to "the spatial tensions" of "the painter's push-pull" surface (135). Perloff writes:

> When these syntactic and prosodic devices are used in conjunction, we get a poetry of great speed, openness, flexibility, and defiance of expectations. Like the "all-over" painting, an O'Hara lyric often seems intentionally deprived of a beginning, middle, and end; it is an instantaneous performance. Syntactic energy is thus equivalent to the painter's "push-pull"—the spatial tensions that keep a surface alive and moving. The rapid cuts from one spatial or temporal zone to another, moreover, give the poetry its peculiar sense of immediacy: everything is absorbed into the NOW. (*FOH*, 135)

Again, Perloff is correct to note that these elements create a certain structural "energy" in O'Hara's poems. However, this energy or tension is also different from the "spatial tensions" of the works of abstract expressionism. First, as noted above, "push-pull" is the use of lines, planes, and colors in painting to either "push" the painting forward or "pull" it backward. The use of two dimensions in painting to create the illusion of a third dimension implicit in the term "push and pull" has no one-to-one parallel with the use of signs to refer to states of affairs. Second, unlike the absence of a coherent image in painting, the use of indeterminate language in a poem to create an incoherent thematic expression tends to slow the reading of a poem down rather than speed it up and absorb the constituent parts of the poem "into the NOW." Poems that use the devices Perloff mentions—"Easter" (1952), *Second Avenue*, and "Biotherm (for Bill Berkson)" (1962), to name a few—are long, difficult works that take time to read and assimilate. Third, to return to the issue of scale: unlike paintings, all of O'Hara's poems have at least a beginning and an end (except for "Poem (WHE EWHEE)" (1950) in which O'Hara parodies Apollinaire's *Calligrammes*), even if we are unable to attach a particular thematic significance to the first or last words of the poem. Thus, unlike a painting, the words of a poem are encountered in a set order. While an individual mark or image on a canvas (such as the letters of the word "SARDINES") acts and reacts with all the other marks or images on a canvas, individual words or phrases in a longer poem, while perhaps acting and reacting in this manner with other words and phrases in close proximity, do not do so with all of the words and phrases of the poem. Furthermore, O'Hara uses other devices besides indeterminate language, including different kinds of allusion, double metaphors, and repetition.

What Perloff does not mention in her application of O'Hara's comments on Pollock to his own work is that O'Hara is simply restating the accepted view of the elements of "surface" and "depth" in Pollock's painting. O'Hara writes, for example, in *Jackson Pollock* (1959):

> Pollock choosing to use no images with real visual equivalents and having not building in mind, struck upon a use of scale which was to have a revolutionary effect on contemporary painting and sculpture. The scale of the painting became that of the painter's body, not the image of a body, and the setting for the scale, which would include all referents, would be the canvas surface itself. Upon this field the physical energies of the artist operate in actual detail, in full scale; the action of inspiration traces its marks of Apelles with no reference to exterior image or environment. It is scale, and no-scale. It is the physical reality of the artist and his activity of expressing it, united to the spiritual reality of the artist in a oneness which has no need for the mediation of metaphor or symbol. It is Action Painting. (*AC*, 34)

What O'Hara notes is that Pollock's choice of scale is not determined by the objects he wishes to represent in his work, because his action paintings are not representations of visual experience at all but rather expressions of the "energies" of the artist himself. O'Hara restates here, for example, Robert Goodnough's claim in "Pollock Paints a Picture" (1951) that artists such as Pollock "are not concerned with representing a preconceived idea, but rather with being involved in an experience of paint and canvas, directly, without interference from the suggested forms and colors of existing objects," and Harold Rosenberg's statement in "The American Action Painters" (1952) that the canvas for Pollock was "an arena in which to act—rather than . . . a space in which to reproduce, re-design, analyze or 'express' an object, actual or imagined."[19]

Beyond Painting

While O'Hara's work is indeed different, this difference is not found in his supposed use of language as paint or espousal of poststructuralist theories of language. Taking O'Hara's literary debt to so-called modern poets more seriously, and providing a more coherent explanation of his relationship with painters such as Picasso, Paul Klee (1879–1940), Max Ernst (1891–1976), Pollock, and Robert Motherwell (1915–91), among others, this work will argue that what distinguishes O'Hara is his radical combination of the notion of writing as an act of exploring his feelings in his work and the emphasis he himself places on the effects of the completed work.[20] As will be shown in chapter 1, in "Memorial Day 1950" (1950), O'Hara draws from expressionist notions of creation, and distinguishes his "messy" poems from the controlled constructivism of other poets and artists. His expressionism is grounded in his love of the material world rather than "in dreams," as it was for the surrealists, and has as its goal the enrichment of our experience of the material world. His poems, O'Hara implies, are like sewage plants. In exploring his feelings in his work, the poet transforms the old, exhausted forms of the self's interaction with the world into new ones that he hopes are "richer than a river" (*CP*, 18).

The purpose of his poems can be characterized in at least two ways. In his "Statement for *The New American Poetry*" (1959), for example, he writes: "It may be that poetry makes life's nebulous events tangible to me and restores their detail; or conversely, that poetry brings forth the intangible quality of incidents which are all too concrete and circumstantial. Or each on specific occasions, or both all the time" (*CP*, 500). On the one hand, then, as we shall see in chapter 3, certain poems are acts of naming the intangible world, with its rapid movements and the constant passing of time, so that moments of experience might be felt in the fullest possible sense. His poems make "life's nebulous events tangible." On the other hand, as we shall see in chapter 2, other poems function to highlight the irreducible nature of experience itself and point to the fact that an effort to organize it into some comprehensive, coherent whole is always reductive, and, for O'Hara, boring as well. It is in this sense that his poems highlight "the intangible quality of incidents" that are "too concrete and circumstantial."

Failure to understand this can lead to a misunderstanding of the value and significance of O'Hara's work. Thus, for example, while Charles Altieri is correct, at least in part, to see in O'Hara's work an emphasis on "radical presence," he defines this as "the insistence that the moment immediately and intensely experienced can restore one to harmony with the world and provide ethical and psychological renewal."[21] O'Hara, however, is not concerned with restoring "harmony," but rather with renewing our interest in our present experience. Therefore, while Altieri provides a number of insightful remarks concerning O'Hara's verse, in the end he faults O'Hara for failing to accomplish objectives that he never set for himself in the first place. Summarizing his treatment of O'Hara, Altieri writes: "His influence and popularity are considerably greater than his achievements—a phenomenon attributable to many factors including his sheer entertainment value and the notoriety of his pathetic and unexpected death."[22] The notion, however, that O'Hara's "entertainment value" is "considerably greater than his achievements" misses the point of much of O'Hara's work and ignores one of O'Hara's principal concerns in it, which is precisely showing us the great value of "entertainment," if we take the word "entertainment" to mean an intense interest in the present moment. For O'Hara, art teaches us how to experience time. O'Hara himself says as much when he writes in "Larry Rivers: A Memoir" (1965) that "[W]hile much of the art of our time has been involved with direct conceptual or ethical considerations, Rivers has chosen to mirror his preoccupations and enthusiasms in an unprogrammatic way." O'Hara concludes that to maintain interest in the present moment is one of the essential values of art: "What his work has always had to say to me, I guess, is to be more keenly interested while I'm still alive. And perhaps this is the most important thing art can say" (*SS*, 171, 173).

Thus, as we shall see in chapter 4, for O'Hara, writing is a testament of the self—of the fact that there is such a thing as the self—but it is not, in addition to this, a means of either discovering some absolute definition of the nature of some essential self or organizing one's experience into some harmonious, coherent whole that can be recognized and comprehended. The self, as an expression of the creative force at work in the world, is irreducible, multiple, and always changing. Thus, unlike other poets in the lyric tradition since Wordsworth, O'Hara does not believe his work can somehow bring him closer to some aboriginal or transhistorical self. Rather, he hopes his work will renew our present experience of the world. It is in this sense, among others, that he characterizes, as we shall see in chapter 1 and in chapter 5, the creative act as an act of love toward the material world.

If what poetry and art teach us is how to feel and how to remain interested in our experience, it is of utmost importance for O'Hara that his poems are, as he writes in relation to Kenneth Koch (1925–2002), "not *dull!*" (*SS*, 60). To fail to engage the interest of others is, for O'Hara, to fail to accomplish one of the basic functions of art. As he writes in "Digression on *Number 1*, 1948" (1956), art is that which reminds us that

> They'll
> never fence the silver range.
> Stars are out and there is sea
> enough beneath the glistening earth

to bear me toward the future
which is not so dark. I see.

(*CP*, 260)

The "silver range" is O'Hara's experience of the world, and poetry and art remind him of what he believes to be the infinite depth of it.

1
"Memorial Day 1950" and the Poetics of Saying "I"

"Memorial Day 1950"

"MEMORIAL DAY 1950" IS ONE OF O'HARA'S MOST IMPORTANT POEMS despite the fact that we only have it today because John Ashbery (b. 1927) copied it out in a letter to Kenneth Koch, who, in turn, sent it to Donald Allen some twenty years later as Allen was preparing the publication of *The Collected Poems of Frank O'Hara.* While it lacks a certain structural coherence, with section breaks and a narrative flow that are evocative of the paragraphs of a prose statement, it functions as a sort of *ars poetica* (*CP*, vii). The poem is one in which O'Hara memorializes heroes of art rather than heroes of war, and eulogizes the concepts of artistic creation he finds in the painting of Picasso, Ernst, and Klee, as well as in the writing of Gertrude Stein (1874–1946), Rimbaud, Auden, Apollinaire, Pasternak, and perhaps both Rilke and Williams as well, thus honoring these artists as having "made" him, while, at the same time, marking them as "dead." He concludes by stating the principal tenet of his own poetics: founded on the notion of love, which, for O'Hara, is a life-giving force, his work complicates, clarifies, and enriches our present experience of the material world.

O'Hara begins the poem with Picasso. In the opening section, he identifies, in language similar to Apollinaire's classic *The Cubist Painters* (1913), Picasso's anti-illusionist, constructivist paintings as marking the beginning of himself as a poet as well as marking the beginning of "modern" man and the "modern" world—a beginning, furthermore, that is created out of the destruction of the old forms of the self's interaction with the world (in this case, the use of perspective in painting). He writes:

> Picasso made me tough and quick, and the world;
> just as in a minute plane trees are knocked down

outside my window by a crew of creators.
Once he got his axe going everyone was upset
enough to fight for the last ditch and heap
of rubbish.

(*CP*, 17)

The "me" of the opening line refers both to Picasso's 1911 painting, *The Poet*, and to O'Hara himself. The painting is composed of shades of brown and gray geometrical planes and straight lines, and Apollinaire describes it in *The Cubist Painters* as being both "honest" in its enumeration of "the elements and details" and "very graceful."[1] Thus, the phrase "Picasso made me tough and quick" refers to Picasso's composition in the painting. Yet, to say that Picasso "made" O'Hara "tough and quick" can mean at least two further things. First, it could be understood to refer to O'Hara's debt to Picasso's style. O'Hara hopes that his poems are, to borrow Apollinaire's words, "honest" and "graceful." As we shall see later in the chapter, O'Hara often used the word "quick" to refer to the honest and passionate expression of feelings in a work of art in response to a moment of crisis, and it is in this sense that art is like war for O'Hara. Second, it could be understood to express a trope that O'Hara would use in his work throughout his life and to which he will return at the end of this poem: that the poet, in exploring himself in his work, becomes a work of art.

In addition to making the poet tough and quick, O'Hara notes that Picasso has "made" the world as well. Here, O'Hara draws from Apollinaire's argument in *The Cubist Painters* that Picasso's paintings are not representations of the "real" world but rather constructs that provide order to otherwise disparate and value free raw feelings.[2] Thus, without artists, Apollinaire writes, "the order we see in nature . . . which is actually no more than an artistic illusion, would immediately vanish. Everything would be reduced to chaos."[3] O'Hara's remark that "plane trees are knocked down / outside my window by a crew of creators" alludes to this destruction of perspective in Picasso's cubist paintings, which do not reproduce the illusion of a traditional third dimension but rather re-create the tactile elements of visual experience. In the poem this act of aggression causes panic as people "fight for the last ditch and heap / of rubbish." What is interesting here, however, is that unlike Apollinaire, O'Hara does not root Picasso's destruction of perspective in ethical considerations alone but also in boredom.[4] If we take the homophone of "plane" in "plain," it points to what O'Hara argues elsewhere in detail: that innovation in art is grounded, among other things, in the artist's boredom with other, more established forms.

At the beginning of the second section, referring to himself as the object of Picasso's "surgery," and thus once again borrowing the language of Apollinaire's *The Cubist Painters* to evoke both the notion that Picasso "made" him and that he himself is a work of art, O'Hara discovers that in his own effort to name experience, he is unable to provide a "language" that rationalizes or names all raw feelings—in particular, the fear of death.[5] He writes:

> Through all that surgery I thought
> I had a lot to say, and named several last things
> Gertrude Stein hadn't had time for; but then
> the war was over, those things had survived
> and even when you're scared art is no dictionary.
> Max Ernst told us that.
>
> (*CP*, 17)

While O'Hara compares his "naming" to Stein's, which in *Tender Buttons* (1914) is akin to cubism's identification of form as that which constructs or mediates feeling, his is an act of saving soon-to-be-dead forms of experience, and, therefore, perhaps more related to Pound's naming in *The Pisan Cantos* (1948), which Ronald Bush has suggested can be understood as a form of saving the poet from oblivion.[6] The poet, however, encounters two problems. The first is that this act of naming seems to be unneeded ("but then / the war was over, those things had survived"). The second is that as meaningful as this naming is, it is unable to name things such as the fear of death ("even when you're scared art is no dictionary"), and, is, therefore, unable to provide a structure or a "language" that is comprehensive or complete.

For O'Hara, art is unable to provide a sign for each form of experience or a structure that might rationalize all our raw feelings—it is, indeed, "no dictionary." O'Hara's reference to Max Ernst in the third section of the poem further emphasizes the notion that art in its enumeration of the world is unable to express a "supreme language." Because of his training in Freudian psychoanalysis, the symbols and images of Ernst's work have often been scoured for the "spiritual sentiment" hidden within them. In his excellent essay on this element of Ernst's work, Werner Spies shows that Ernst invites such scouring in order to frustrate it. Spies argues that in creating images whose meaning is "overdetermined"—packed with so much suggestive and disparate psychoanalytical grist—all psychological mills become overloaded.[7] Spies concludes that "the repeatedly advanced comparison between Ernstian 'collage work' and Freudian 'dream work' proves misleading, a deceptive model for interpretation."[8]

In his early poem "Meditations on Max Ernst's *Histoire Naturelle*" (1950), O'Hara sees in Ernst's work both a rejection of the facile psychological reading of the artist's images and a rejection of the hope that, in providing images or words that were understood to function as a language of the mind, artists might be able to provide a language of the mind that, in turn, could be scrutinized for clues as to the meaning and nature of the self. He reads Ernst's symbols as emblems of the power and beauty of the material world, which the artist uses to enlarge our *experiential* knowledge of the world itself. In a gloss on one of the prints, O'Hara writes:

> It is true that ferocious lions, all lions, scent succulence, and one may add scent succulence lasciviously, delicious word. It is also true that at the same time lime trees grow tractably, especially on the boarded plains, and most especially when within hearing of the sniffing lions. But no matter what happens we, as vegetable spirits, fall to our knees before the beauty of nature (how we sniff and enlarge our sensibility!) because of nature and our knowledge of nature
>
> (*EW*, 91).

While O'Hara drops the word "beauty" from his poems and criticism after 1950, the point here is that O'Hara does not see in Ernst's work either a transcendental world evoked in his almost mythological images or the expression of the code of the unconscious mind, but rather a renewal of our existential knowledge of the world in the bringing together of contrasting shapes and images, in this case, lions smelling "succulence" and trees growing "tractably" against the "boarded plains."

This realization that art cannot provide an alphabet of the mind that can be scrutinized for residual "spiritual sentiment" (to use Georges Braque's term) is first experienced as loss by the poet. Having learned from Max Ernst that "art is no dictionary," the lesson is perhaps compounded in Picasso's *Guernica* (1937):

> How many trees and frying pans
> I loved and lost! Guernica hollered look out!
> but we were all busy hoping our eyes were talking

> to Paul Klee. My mother and father asked me and
> I told them from my tight blue pants we should
> love only the stones, the sea, and heroic figures.
> Wasted child! I'll club you on the shins! I
> wasn't surprised when the older people entered
> my cheap hotel room and broke my guitar and my can
> of blue paint.
>
> (*CP*, 17)

Picasso's *Guernica*, painted in response to Hitler's bombing of the small Basque town on April 27, 1937, and first appearing at the Spanish Pavilion of the Exposition internationale des arts et techniques dans la vie moderne, was presented as a warning against the dangers of fascism. However, Picasso's *Guernica* also has radical aesthetic implications, and it is important to note that the poet's response in "Memorial Day 1950" is not political, but artistic. After all, the painting hollers "look out!" while the poet and his unidentified companions are "hoping" their eyes are "talking / to Paul Klee."

It is difficult to say what comparison O'Hara might be drawing here between Picasso's *Guernica* and Klee's painting, if any. There are, however, a number of notable differences between *Guernica* and Klee's work. One is the size of *Guernica.* It is one of Picasso's largest works, covering some 292 square feet, and it functions both as a monument against the bombing in Guernica itself and as a form of attack against war and violence in general.[9] A second is its darker colors, crossing diagonal lines, and overlapping planes, which are different from Klee's somewhat more decorative small, colorful landscapes composed of geometrical shapes. While Klee understood artistic creation in expressionist terms, his work shows, perhaps, much more control than Picasso's seemingly messier *Guernica.*

A further difference between Picasso and Klee might be found in Picasso's characterization of painting as "an instrument of war."[10] The idea that art is "an instrument of war" can mean a number of things, but for Picasso it refers specifically to the idea that art should not be created "to decorate apartments"; rather it should be used in "attack and defense against the enemy," which, in this case, was the rising fascist regime of Hitler.[11] This is somewhat different from Klee's idea that art takes us "deep down to the source of all."[12] Klee understood artistic creation to be an expression of the life force that is at work in the material world, even if he claimed that this force "cannot be named."[13]

Whatever the source of O'Hara's interest in *Guernica*, the painting marks a shift in the poet's perception of art. In an ironic reversal of Mayakovsky's later rejection by Communist youth for his "unintelligible" poetry and seeming lack of commitment to "heroic figures," the poet here is punished by "the older people" for his bold statement that "we should / love only the stones, the sea, and heroic figures."[14] Out of this moment of loss, in which the specter of Picasso's earlier work is nevertheless present in the broken pieces of guitar and blue paint, the poet emerges with a new view of artistic creation—one that is understood as a messy, violent exploration. Evoking the work of both Rimbaud and Auden, O'Hara states: "all of us began to think / with our bare hands and even with blood all over / them"; and he claims that "we never / smeared anything except to find out how it lived." While the "smearing" here is no less destructive than cubism's earlier destruction of perspective, it is messier—more akin to fighting and the messiness of war than to Picasso's earlier neat "surgery."

O'Hara's expressionist poetics is stated even more clearly elsewhere in his work. In "To Gottfried Benn" (1958), for example, O'Hara writes that "Poetry is not instruments," but that

> like the passion of a nation
> at war it moves quickly
> provoked to defense or aggression
> unreasoning power
> an instinct for self-declaration. . . .
>
> (*CP*, 309–10)

Poetic creation, therefore, is not the result of the rational application of formal tools, but, like acts of war, quick and passionate—so quick, in fact, that it is not that different from instinct. However, unlike rash decisions to go to war, the quickness of poetic composition, for O'Hara, is what assures it of its integrity. This is because the quick expression of feeling, for O'Hara, is a more honest expression, and, therefore, a "truer" creative form.

This, of course, is not a new understanding of poetic creation. For example, compositional speed is one of the cornerstones of Pasternak's aesthetic.[15] Pasternak's friend and correspondent, Marina Tsvetaeva, defines artistic speed as that which is so great it seems to annihilate time. She writes in "Art in the Light of Conscience" (1932): "A reflex before any thought, even before any feeling, the deepest and fastest—as by electric current—spearing of the whole being by a given phenomenon, and the simultaneous, almost preceding it, answer to it."[16] In the visual arts, furthermore, the notion that the artist might be able to recapture what John Ruskin (1819–1900) called the "innocent eye" of childhood, (which is, as Pepe Karmel notes, visual experience before it becomes "translated" into the "language of three-dimensional form and space") is something that links the innovations of the impressionists to those of the cubists and surrealists.[17]

What O'Hara points out in "To Gottfried Benn," however, as well as in "Memorial Day 1950," is that this exploration of feeling in art is not as neat or as clean as it is presented in Benn's poems. O'Hara goes on to say in "To Gottfried Benn":

> like nations its faults are absorbed
> in the heat of sides and angles
> combatting the void of rounds
> a solid of imperfect placement
>
> (*CP*, 310)

Art is messy and imperfect. It is a passionate search for a gesture that will combat "the void of rounds," which is, perhaps, the nebulous or circular nature of what we call the self. This gesture, however, is not one that will comprehend the void. It is, rather, "a solid of imperfect placement." Unable to capture the total void, the artist is nevertheless able to create a provisional "solid," which functions as an "imperfect" but tangible expression of the individual self.

Furthermore, while O'Hara does not claim that this exploration will provide him with an alphabet of the mind or a Mallarméan "supreme language," this does not mean, as is clear from his comments in "To Gottfried Benn," that poetry is meaningless, or that it is a form of pure play. In "Memorial Day 1950," for example, the poet learns a number of smaller, but no less important, things about the world and himself. He learns that poetry is not "crap," and, as becomes clear at the end of the poem, that crap is not crap, either.[18] He learns from Rilke, perhaps, that dolls signify death; from Ernst that "art is no dictionary"; and from Pasternak, as we will discuss below, that art is love.[19] Indeed, O'Hara's own emphasis on renewing our present experience of the world is based on a certain *understanding* of the world and of the nature of human experience and, therefore, purports to "teach" us, among other things, that experience is irreducible and paratactical and that our longing for love seems to be both natural and always unfulfilled. While O'Hara is not the most political of poets, he does not avoid political subject matter. The principal purpose of his work, however, remains to reinvigorate our present experience of the world.

In the next section of the poem, O'Hara distinguishes his understanding of exploration from that of the surrealists. While the surrealists were committed to exploring the mind's subconsciousness in the hope that in coupling irrational dreams and rational experience the artist might at last reveal in his art what André Breton calls a "superior reality," O'Hara roots his exploration in love.[20] O'Hara writes:

> Our responsibilities did not begin
> in dreams, though they began in bed. Love is first of all
> a lesson in utility. I hear the sewage singing
> underneath my bright white toilet seat and know
> that somewhere sometime it will reach the sea:
> gulls and swordfishes will find it richer than a river.
> And airplanes are perfect mobiles, independent
> of the breeze; crashing in flames they show us how
> to be prodigal. O Boris Pasternak, it may be silly
> to call to you, so tall in the Urals, but your voice
> cleans our world, clearer to us than the hospital:
> you sound above the factory's ambitious gargle.
> Poetry is as useful as a machine!
>
> (*CP*, 17–18)

As David LeHardy Sweet notes, love is one of the aspects of O'Hara's poetics that distinguishes him both from the French surrealists and from his contemporaries—as well as from, it should be added, pure formalists.[21] The notion that artistic creation is an act of love is something that O'Hara perhaps learned from Pasternak's *Safe Conduct* (1930). For Pasternak, the mind and the material world are not two distinct entities. The goal of the artist, therefore, is not to break through the perceptual world to some unseen "superior," and somehow more real, world—whether it is conceived of as the unconscious mind or absolute Spirit—but rather to express the great force of feeling he finds within himself in order to renew our experience of the "turgid," half-forgotten things of the material world.[22] This transference is what Pasternak characterizes as an act of love. In an important passage in *Safe Conduct*, Pasternak describes the artist himself as moving ahead at great speed, which is to say, he is experiencing the present moment with great intensity. However, aware that all of life is not moving forward with him, the artist experiences a desire (which, for

Pasternak, is artistic inspiration) to look back on these "turgid," half-forgotten things. The artist includes them in his work, thus setting them in motion again. This, for Pasternak, is an act of love, in which the artist transfers, and therefore transforms, objects from a half-dead (immobile) existence to one that is full of "being" and life, and it is in this sense that art completes, or brings into a renewed existence, objects of the material world.[23]

O'Hara shares Pasternak's understanding of artistic creation as rooted in a love for the seemingly "turgid" things of world, which, it is worth noting, is an understanding of art that Pasternak himself perhaps assimilated from Rilke's *Notebooks of Malte Laurids Brigge* (1910). Rilke, in turn, followed the Baudelaire of "Une charogne" (1857), who, as Eudo Mason notes, "saw a great affirmation of life through the transfiguring power of the poetic word, just at the point where life is most horrifying and disgusting."[24] However, while Pasternak's concept of love can, at times, be likened, as Angela Livingstone points out, to "a Dionysian frenzy," O'Hara figures love as "a lesson in utility."[25] While O'Hara would sometimes embellish this notion of love with comparisons of the poet's love to perverse images of the sacrificial love of Christ, in "Memorial Day," following Rilke and D. H. Lawrence (1885–1930), O'Hara underscores art's similarities to sex in its finite mechanics, as well as in its production of pleasure. Love leads to sex, and sex leads to both pleasure and the reproduction of the species, which is "useful" in that it propagates life and maintains human existence. In this sense, love is not so different in its mechanics from the mechanics of the digestive system that takes food, processes it, and reintroduces into the natural world, where it helps to sustain the life of "gulls and swordfishes" who find it "richer than a river."

This is the subject of one O'Hara's earliest long poems,"Oranges: 12 Pastorals." In "Oranges," the poet looks at the natural world, mixing images of sex and filth with images of Greek deities (Orpheus, Pan, and snakes) and Catholicism (the Holy Ghost, Judas Agonistes, Black Mass), and states at the end of the poem: "This is the miracle: that our elegant invention the natural / world redeems by filth" (*CP*, 9). The filth in the poem is both human excrement and the dirt produced from dead bodies, which gives life to trees and plants. O'Hara understands both Greek mythology and the story of the death and resurrection of Christ to be based on what is, for him, the fact of the circle of life—birth, death, rebirth. He sees art to be based on this same fact. He therefore, takes on the persona of a sort of Nietzschean Antichrist in the middle of the eleventh section of the poem. This persona, "wrapped in jungle leaves" and riding on a "zebra through the scrubby / plains which nevertheless now and then bloom with cattleyas and blue hydrangeas," ironically speaks of the beauty within himself. However, unlike Rilke's sometime Christlike persona, O'Hara is not entirely sure of himself. The beauty within him "withers" at a glance, after which the poet loses all composure:

> Bring me my doll: I must make contact with something dead.
> And now that I am initiated I have only to bury you, my dear doll, before
> I set out. Here beneath this yew I dig a hole for wooden playthings. Man is
> nothing but this doggy instinct
> Kiss me, kiss me! doll!
> I smother!
>
> (*CP*, 8)

Paranoid about his creative powers, the poet must make contact with death, thus placing himself in touch with the circle of birth-death-rebirth that is the foundation of life. In doing so, he finds that the fear of death, figured in the burying of the doll, is, in fact, based on a love of life, or a need to remain in contact with the material world, a need that, in the poem, can be observed in the poet's sudden felt need for love ("Kiss me, kiss me! doll!).

The notion that art is akin both to sex and the mechanics of the digestive tract is evoked again and again in O'Hara's work. In "Ode on Saint Cecilia's Day" (1950), for example, which is a response to John Dryden's "A Song for St. Cecilia's Day" (1687), O'Hara compares the mechanical music of Saint Cecilia to the passionate notes of Pan's sexual longing and concludes: "Fie, Cecilia! / your instrument / will never lead us in war or love!" (*CP*, 29). In "Easter" (1952), the poet becomes the redeemer of the natural world in "playing" with filth; and in "Meditations in an Emergency" (1954), "the heart" is where "the filth is pumped in and slanders and pollutes." In the end, the heart becomes a "greenhouse" (*CP*, 96–100, 197). In "To the Mountains in New York" (1954), O'Hara writes: "I feel the earth pulsing against my heart. / They call me The Dirt Eater. The Gambler" (*CP*, 200). While the weight of the dirt prevents the poet (here figured as a snake) from rising from the ground ("I can't rise, I'm so filthy! so heavy!"), he grows trees and flowers that rise from the ground once he possesses his "full stench" (*CP*, 200). In "Spleen" (1954), O'Hara compares writing to "vomiting," while in "Ode on Causality" (1958) he hopes to inscribe "a sexual bliss" on "the page of whatever energy I burn for art" (CP, 302). In each case, the act of creation is an act of love of the material world that is akin to the mechanics of the digestive track.

In the final section of "Memorial Day 1950," we return to the "hotel room" of the third section, and all of the theories of artistic creation are present as the poem finishes in a final flourish:

> Look at my room.
> Guitar strings hold up pictures. I don't need
> a piano to sing, and naming things is only the intention
> to make things. A locomotive is more melodious
> than a cello. I dress in oil cloth and read music
> by Guillaume Apollinaire's clay candelabra. Now
> my father is dead and has found out you must look things
> in the belly, not in the eye. If only he had listened
> to the men who made us, hollering like stuck pigs!
>
> (*CP*, 18)

Here O'Hara restates his understanding of artistic creation as a form of expression. The notion of art as construction is present in O'Hara's allusion to the guitar that recurs in Braque and Picasso and in the phrase "naming things is only the intention / to make things," which might possibly refer to Williams's notion of a work of art as a constructed material object not different in kind from other material objects. (In his introduction to *The Wedge* (1944), for example, Williams writes: "A poem is a small (or large) machine made of words."[26]) The notion of art as a form of self-exploration is evoked in the figure of the poet dressing himself "in oil cloth" and reading "music / by Guillaume Apollinaire's clay candelabra," which refers to a painting that Apollinaire mentions in *The Cubist Painters.* Claiming that art can contain anything, Apollinaire writes that he has even seen "earthenware candelabras which were to be stuck to a canvas so that they seemed to protrude from inside it."[27] O'Hara, however, takes Apollinaire's argument a step further, wrapping himself in "oil cloth" and becoming a work of art himself.

The poem, thus, has come full circle, as O'Hara's best poems tend to do. The poet is figured as a work of art in his possible reference to Picasso's *The Poet* at the beginning of the poem, and now he wraps himself in "oil cloth" and reads "music / by Guillaume Apollinaire's clay candelabra." Here O'Hara states: "you must look things / in the belly, not in the eye." While the meaning of this phrase is unclear, it makes the most sense to understand this as a distinction between O'Hara's own notion of artistic creation that is founded on love and whose purpose is to produce an emotional, even corporeal, effect in us (looking things "in the belly") and art's preoccupation with enumerating observable experience (looking things "in the eye") (*CP*, 499). Thus, O'Hara imagines that, like his actual father, his metaphorical fathers—the artists named in the poem—have learned that death frustrates all such possible insights and all such hopes.[28] "In Memorial Day 1950," therefore, in addition to drawing the distinction between himself and his artistic and literary fathers, O'Hara's final section can be understood as an imaginative reconciliation with his father, where his father comes to agree with his son after his death that death is indeed inexplicable and that it is better to serve one's pleasures than to serve some philosophical or religious structure that tries to organize the world into a coherent whole.[29]

While "Memorial Day" is one of O'Hara's first poems in which he treats his own aesthetics, it is far from brash and confident. The shadow of failure permeates the poem. Throughout, the poet gets it wrong. While at the end of the poem he resolves to "look life in the belly" rather than "in the eye," the number of past failures indicates that this may prove to be but one more misstep. In this sense, it is interesting to compare the poem with "February" (1951), which was written less than a year after "Memorial Day." In it, as in "Memorial Day," the poet is presented as a child in love with foreign art that leads him to experience a sort of artistic breakthrough: he comes to understand art as an "excess of / love." In "February," however, O'Hara upbraids himself for his failure to write in these "New metrics":

> The scene is the same,
> and though I try to imagine
> plinking starry guitars,
>
> and while I spend my
> time listening to a foreign
> contralto sing the truth,
>
> the earth is everywhere,
> brown and aching. At first
> it seemed that this life

would be different: born
again in someone else's
arms, after seasons of childhood

and error and defense,
I thought freshly and tried
to change the color of my

habit. New metrics would be
mine in this excess of
love! but I was a braggart

to hope so. My old hurts
kept attacking me at odd
moments, after too many

songs, on public conveyances,
in the blue light of bars. Ah!

(*CP*, 53)

The notion that "New metrics would be / mine in this excess of / love!" is evocative of O'Hara's understanding in "Memorial Day" of artistic exploration grounded in love. However, while in "Memorial Day" O'Hara goes on to claim that "gulls and swordfishes will find" his new poems "richer than a river," here, he states, "I was a braggart / to hope so."

Despite the self-confidence he might have projected to friends such as Joe LeSueur, O'Hara would struggle throughout his life with the question of whether his work was good or not.[30] Yet, he never repudiated the idea that writing was an act of constructive exploration akin to love and that the purpose of creating objects of art was to heighten and nuance our present experience of the world. Even in "February," he ends the poem with a renewed commitment to continue to write poems in his "New metrics," whatever the response of the critics or the general public:

I cried, do not blame me,

save your temper for the
others! and at the same instant
in the same breath cried,

break me! I dare you, for
which of us am I? you will
break yourself! . . .

(*CP*, 53–54)

That O'Hara maintained this poetics is most evident in his statements on his work, in which, despite his minimization of the value of such statements, he discusses his principal presuppositions regarding the nature of artistic creation and the nature and value of art itself. A brief examination of these three statements, as well as his sole recorded interview, will show that O'Hara continued to conceive of artistic creation as an act of self-exploration, whose principal purpose is not to define or express some universal self, but rather to create an artifact that enriches our present experience of the material world.

O'Hara's Statements

O'Hara tended to avoid writing or talking about his poetry. During his lifetime, he made two direct statements on his own work, wrote one letter explaining that he could not, in fact, give such a statement, and had one long interview with Edward Lucie-Smith the year before he died in 1965. The first two statements—"Personism: A Manifesto" (1959) and "Statement for *The New American Poetry*" (1959)—were written at the request of Donald Allen to be included in *The New American Poetry* (1960), but were, O'Hara later claimed, more "a diary of my thoughts" ("Personism") and a "diary of a particular day and the depressed mood of that day" ("Statement for *The New American Poetry*") than expressions of his poetics (*CP*, 510–11). The third, "Statement for Paterson Society" (1961), was a letter in response to Paterson Society's request for a statement (*CP*, 510).

O'Hara's reluctance to provide a statement of his work can be attributed to at least two converging factors. First, as Perloff remarks, O'Hara viewed such statements as "unnecessarily labored accounts of the poetic process" (*FOH*, 18). In his interview with Edward Lucie-Smith, O'Hara claims that the stylistic innovations of the avant-garde were not so much a reaction against "the bourgeoisie" as they were a reaction against boredom. Following, perhaps, Larry Rivers's comment three years earlier in an interview with O'Hara that the "history of art and the history of each artist's development are the response to the discomforts of boredom," O'Hara states: "It has been made up completely, and all through history, with people who are bored by other people's ideas" (*AC*, 113; *SS*, 9). He continues

> L-S: This is a kind of dynamic of impatience which you're proposing.
> O'H: Yes, and boredom. Western civilization, however, has really put, laid[,] an awful load on that thing because so many things have already been done. What would you do that would be different and not boring?
> L-S: You think it's important to be new then?
> O'H: No, I think it's very important not to be bored though.
>
> (*SS*, 9)

Furthermore, refuting the theories that "happenings" were "existential" or "propaganda" for some movement, O'Hara claims:

> Happenings is [*sic*] just like a little play. There's nothing mysterious about it at all. They never were anything more than that and the whole mystique of them is absolute nonsense. They're improvised plays. Everybody's done them, and done them, and you've done them yourself as a child. They're always—that was their great charm, that they just happened because somebody wanted to do them and they wanted to invite a few people who usually came to the gallery, or whom you liked to come and see them. It always was. The Jim Dine ones, the Oldenburg ones, the Red Grooms ones—they were always done in a certain manner of "I'm going to do this delightful thing, I think, and I hope you'll come and think it's delightful." . . . It's supposed to remind you that art is fun and that we're all children and that it's marvelous. That's all they meant by them. It is not existential, you know, or propaganda for any movement. (*SS*, 16–17)

While there is a clear element of provocation in these comments, O'Hara debunks what he sees to be overly complex and high-sounding explanations of artistic innovation. For him, avoiding boredom is a sufficiently serious explanation of such innovations. If art does not disclose the meaning of our experience, or organize it into a form that makes rational sense of it, it must, at least, make us "more keenly interested" in it (*SS*, 173). To be boring, however, is to fail to do this. This is why, for O'Hara, avoiding boredom is more important than being new. While it is, perhaps, impossible to entirely avoid being boring without also being new, being new is not in itself enough to postpone boredom. Hence, for O'Hara, the question is: "What would you do that would be different and not boring?"

O'Hara wanted to remain unassociated with a particular "school" of poetry. While O'Hara wrote a letter to Paterson Society explaining his reasons for not providing a statement, in the end he did not send it, as Donald Allen notes, perhaps because even in the form of a refusal the letter might have been understood as a statement (as it indeed has), thus aligning his work too closely with the work of Allen Ginsberg (1926–97) and other Beat poets who had a close association with the Paterson Society (*CP*, 558). O'Hara liked Ginsberg and his work, but he was less fond of his touting of a so-called new poetry, as he noted, in a letter to Kenneth Koch on January 19, 1957.

That O'Hara was keen to remain unassociated with a particular "school" of poetry is even clearer in his interview with Edward Lucie-Smith. To Lucie-Smith's question on the position of his work vis-à-vis "the academic and Black Mountain, or between Lowell and Olson," O'Hara responds that there is no relation whatsoever: "Actually I don't really see what my relation is to them one way or the other except that we all live at the same time" (*SS*, 12–13).

Nevertheless, O'Hara wrote three statements on his work. The first is the parodic but nevertheless serious "Personism: A Manifesto."

"Personism: A Manifesto"

"Personism," was not included in Allen's volume because, as O'Hara informs us in his letter to Paterson Society, Allen suggested that it was "unwise to use it in relation to the earlier poems included" (*CP*, 511). While this may be true, it may also be that it was too parodic with respect to the other statements that would be included in the volume.

Given his antagonism to such statements, O'Hara begins "Personism" with an explanation of his reasons for writing a statement at all:

> Everything is in the poems, but at the risk of sounding like the poor wealthy man's Allen Ginsberg I will write to you because I just heard that one of my fellow poets thinks that a poem of mine that can't be got at one reading is because I was confused too. Now, come on. I don't believe in god, so I don't have to make elaborately sounded structures. I hate Vachel Lindsay, always have; I don't even like rhythm, assonance, all that stuff. You just go on your nerve. If someone's chasing you down the street with a knife you just run, you don't turn around and shout, "Give it up! I was a track star for Mineola Prep." (*CP*, 498)

He is not writing, in other words, to explain his work, but to correct a misconception of it. That misconception is that one of his poems is difficult to understand because he himself was "confused." (O'Hara does not tell us which poem this was, though it may very well have been *Second Avenue.* The fact that one of the principal subjects of "Personism" is abstraction and the fact that O'Hara refers to Allen Ginsberg's comments on the abstraction of *Second Avenue* in the journal *It Is* both point to it as the poem in question.) O'Hara argues in these opening lines, and more fully in the rest of the statement that the remark that his poems cannot be understood because he himself is "confused" is based on a misconception of what art should do. He also argues that the abstraction or obscure nature of his poems is the result of his emotional involvement with and response to the world, rather than the result of a commitment to a predetermined style based on ideological considerations.

While "Personism" is clearly parodic, it is more than a mere tongue-in-cheek response to what he sees as belabored accounts of writing. O'Hara first corrects the view that a poem is meant to "improve" one's audience. He writes:

> But how can you really care if anybody gets it, or gets what it means, or if it improves them. Improves them for what? For death? Why hurry them along? Too many poets act like a middle-aged mother trying to get her kids to eat too much cooked meat, and potatoes with drippings (tears). I don't give a damn whether they eat or not. Forced feeding leads to excessive thinness (effete). Nobody should experience anything they don't need to, if they don't need poetry bully for them. I like the movies too. (*CP*, 498)

Later in the statement, O'Hara contrasts this understanding of a poem as a message that "improves" one's audience to his own understanding of a poem as a telephone call to a loved one, whose meaning is located in the expressive act of the call itself as well as in its propositional content. It is not that a phone call to a loved one lacks representational content, but rather that the meaning of the call cannot be reduced to the meaning of the words spoken in the call—which, if one is calling a loved one, can be rather banal so long as those words afford the occasion to be with that person. Like a poem, the phone call is valued to a large extent not for what it represents but for what it is itself and, in this sense, exists as an irreducible, autonomous event. So too, O'Hara implies, do his poems.

O'Hara states in his letter to the Paterson Society that his style of writing is not related to a particular theoretical or ideological commitment, but rather to his exploration of his feelings in language itself. It is not so much that O'Hara believes he does not have such commitments, but rather that his commitments concern less a *style* than a *process*. Hence, O'Hara claims that the source of his abstract language is not found in his ideological presuppositions, but in his immediate emotional response to the world around him. This is the point he makes when he distinguishes between running and shouting when someone is chasing you. To run is to see the form of a poem as an animate response to the pressing emotional needs of a particular moment. To shout is to have a disinterested intellectual preoccupation with the technicalities of style (as well as to attract attention to one's relative skill in mastering these technicalities). The language and form of his poems, O'Hara implies, are the end results of his emotional involvement and response to the world around him rather than the result of disinterested speculation.

In the penultimate paragraph of "Personism," O'Hara compares abstraction in painting and abstraction in poetry. He writes:

> Abstraction (in poetry, not in painting) involves personal removal by the poet. For instance, the decision involved in the choice between "the nostalgia *of* the infinite" and "the nostalgia *for* the infinite" defines an attitude towards degree of abstraction. The nostalgia *of* the infinite representing the greater degree of abstraction, removal, and negative capability (as in Keats and Mallarmé). Personism, a movement which I recently founded and which nobody knows about, interests me a great deal, being so totally opposed to this kind of abstract removal that it is verging on a true abstraction for the first time, really, in the history of poetry. (*CP*, 498)

Abstraction in poetry is most often the result of the objectification of experience. That is, it is the result of experience considered apart from its occurrence in a particular moment of time and in the mind of a particular individual. Personal experience, in this sense, is treated as somehow existing outside the mind of the poet, toward which he assumes the position of disinterested observer. Hence, the reason that "the nostalgia *of* the infinite" is more abstract than "the nostalgia *for* the infinite" is that the preposition "for" implies that someone feels nostalgic, whereas the preposition "of" does not. Abstraction in the painting of Jackson Pollock, however, does not involve such a "personal removal," but rather is a result of his exploring his experience in the materials of the medium, and this is the sort of abstraction that O'Hara hopes is present in his own work (*AC*, 13).

Furthermore, like Jackson Pollock's completed abstractions, the purpose of the exploration of his experience in O'Hara's poems is not to come to terms with the meaning of his experience, if the word "meaning" is used to refer to the idea that his experience is part of, or determined by, some extraexperiential telos, but rather to provide his experience with a form that, as an artifact, produces an emotional response in others. Discussing the use of scale in Pollock's paintings, O'Hara, as was noted in the introduction, claims that the size of Pollock's paintings has to do with the "energies" or emotions of the artist himself. O'Hara writes: "Scale, that mysterious and ambiguous quality in art which elsewhere is a simple designation, has a particular significance in Pollock's work, but it has nothing to do with perspectival relationships in the traditional sense or with the relationship of the size of the object painted to the size of the object in reality. It has to do, rather, with the emotional effect of the painting upon the spectator" (*AC*, 34). It is the physical qualities of size, and, we can assume, the color and texture of Pollock's work, rather than the discursive content of the figurative images, that evoke an emotional response in the viewers of it.

This is an understanding of art that O'Hara would repeat with respect to other artists throughout his life, and is the source of O'Hara's numerous comments against subject matter. In 1948, for example, he writes that "there is no subject of true literature" (*EW*, 104), and in 1953, in a letter to an editor explaining the subject matter of the poem *Second Avenue*, he writes that the subject matter of the poem "is beside the poem's point in most cases" (*CP*, 495). Four years later, he expresses much the same aversion in more forceful terms when he writes in his poem "To Hell with It" (1957), "How I hate subject matter!" (*CP*, 275). Works created in order to represent a particular subject, he explains in his journal in 1948, "can never be more than what they set out to do" and are the works of the "inferior artist" (*EW*, 103). The true artist "must think only of and for the emergent work and not allow messages or ideas as such to displace the validity of the work with their sham importance and subtle derangement of emphasis" (*EW*, 103). In these passages, O'Hara does not claim that his poems do not have subject matter, but rather that while present, the expression of subject matter in terms of rational propositional statements is not the principal purpose of the poem. Rather, it is to produce an emotional effect on the audience.

"Statement for *The New American Poetry*"

In the short "Statement for *The New American Poetry*," which did appear in Allen's *New American Poetry*, O'Hara again addresses the question of the relationship of his experience to the language and form of his poems, and, in turn, the function, or aesthetic value, of his work, which he identifies in terms of its effect on his perception of the world. He writes: "I am mainly preoccupied with the world as I experience it, and at times when I would rather be dead the thought that I could never write another poem has so far stopped me. . . . What is happening to me, allowing for lies and exaggerations which I try to avoid, goes into my poems" (*CP*, 500). The first thing to note is that, for O'Hara, his experience is the source of his poems. That O'Hara's experience "goes into" his poems, and is present in his poems, he writes later in the statement, "in whatever form" he can find it, implies an expressionist understanding of writing. Furthermore, the comment that he tries to avoid "lies and exaggerations" further implies that the act of writing for him is one of expression rather than construction or representation—however close these words might be in meaning.

His view that part of the artistic act of creation is, indeed, expression is further compounded in his comments on Olson and Pound's poems later in the same interview. O'Hara remarks:

> [I]f you want to talk about it [style] in Olson's poems or Ezra Pound's, it comes from the breath of the person just as a stroke of paint comes from the wrist and hand and arm and shoulder and all that of the painter. So therefore the point is really more to establish one's own measure and breath in poetry, I think, than—this sounds wildly ambitious since I don't think I've done it but I think that great poets do do it—rather than fitting your ideas into an established order, syllabically and phonetically and so on. I think certain poets have been very much inspired by American painting. You know, not in the sense of subject matter, or anything like that, but in the ambition to be that, to be the work yourself, and therefore accomplish it. (*SS*, 17)

The idea that style comes from "the breath of the person" is a restatement of Olson's claim in "Projective Verse" (1951) that "the line comes (I swear it) from the breath, from the breathing, of the man who writes it."[31] For O'Hara, however, "breath" does not refer to the breath that comes from the lungs, as it does for Olson, but rather is a metaphor for the poet himself, which is the sole root of his stylistic and formal decisions.

While the source of O'Hara's style is this exploration of his experience, he does not believe that the form discovered in this will provide his experience with an ultimate value or absolute meaning. He writes: "I don't think my experiences are clarified or made beautiful for myself or anyone else; they are just there in whatever form I can find them. . . . It may be that poetry makes life's nebulous events tangible to me and restores their detail; or conversely, that poetry brings forth the intangible quality of incidents which are all too concrete and circumstantial. Or each on specific occasions, or both all the time" (*CP*, 500).

This is evocative of Rilke's remark that his poems express "what goes on half-consciously within and can hardly be said really to happen at all," and of Pasternak, when he distinguishes art from science in that while science is concerned with "principle and numbers, which express the permanent or repeatable qualities of things, art deals with the unique and transient 'presence' of something, its 'voice,' what it *feels* like, *now*." O'Hara identifies the value of his work as providing intangible events with a certain concreteness and as providing events that are "all too concrete" with a certain ethereal, intangible, otherness.[32]

"Statement for Paterson Society"

O'Hara's final statement is not a statement at all, but a letter to Elsa Dorfman's Paterson Society. In this letter, however, O'Hara nevertheless makes a number of remarks on his work. One is that his poems are autonomous objects—objects whose raison d'être is not to represent but to *be*—whose "effect" cannot be captured in poetic statements or theoretical explanations. O'Hara writes, for example, that if he were to describe "the effect other things have had upon me which I in my more day-dreamy moments wish that I could effect in others," such a description would always fall short of capturing the exact effect he hopes is produced in his work (*CP*, 510). This is because, he implies, the exact effect a poem produces is proper to the poem itself:

> Well you can't have a statement saying "My poetry is the Sistine Chapel of verse," or "My poetry is just like Pollock, de Kooning and Guston rolled into one great verb," or "My poetry is like a windy day on a hill overlooking the stormy ocean"—first of all it isn't so far as I can tell, and secondly even if it were something like all of these that wouldn't be because I managed to make it that way. I couldn't, it must have been an accident, and I would probably not recognize it myself. Further, what would poetry like that be? It would have to be the Sistine Chapel itself, the paintings themselves, the day and time specifically. Impossible. (*CP*, 510)

In addition to once again asserting the differences between the arts—this time including architecture as well as painting and poetry—O'Hara, notes that the effects his poems produce are sui generis. The effect of each poem is original to the poem itself. Hence, all attempts to explain or describe it with a simile or metaphor are always imprecise. Furthermore, to explain his work would be to "kill" it, because it would dull the experiential effect of his work, which, for O'Hara, is the principal vehicle of meaning: "I don't want to make up a lot of prose about something that is perfectly clear in the poems. If you cover someone with earth and grass grows, you don't know what they looked like any more. Critical prose makes too much grass grow, and I don't want to help hide my own poems, much less kill them" (*CP*, 510). To explain his work, in other words, would remove the need of the audience to engage with the work itself and therefore experience the pleasurable benefits of grappling with the structural conundrum presented in the materials of the medium. While O'Hara does not make the explicit statement that his poems are autonomous objects here, he implies as much. The underlying assumption in his remark that the effect his poems produce is sui generis is that the poems themselves are, indeed, autonomous objects. In fact, it is impossible, it seems, to claim the former without, in turn, implying the latter.

Another reason that O'Hara gives for not providing Paterson Society with a statement of his work is that he does not have a single "style." O'Hara writes, for example, that if instead of describing the effect he hopes his poems produce, he were to explain the technical aspects of his work—"my convictions concerning form, measure, sound, yardage, placement and ear"—not only would such an explanation remove the pleasure of experiencing his poems at first hand from those who read his work, but it would provide little insight into his work as a whole, because, he claims, such formal aspects change from one poem to the next (*CP*, 510). He writes: "I can't think of any more than one poem at a time, so I would end up with a 'poetics' based on one of my poems which any other poem of mine would completely contradict except for certain affections or habits of speech they might include. So that would be of no use for general readers, and misleading for anyone who had already read any of my poems. So, as they say in the Café Flore, it's better to *tas* [*sic*] *gueule* (*CP*, 510). While it is not true that O'Hara's "affections" or "habits of speech" remain constant throughout his work while his formal "convictions" vary—his formal decisions are as constant, and as variable, as his "affections" or "habits of speech"—the point O'Hara makes here is that he has no predetermined convictions concerning the use or nonuse of particular formal elements in his work.

This is something that O'Hara states on more than one occasion in his discussion of the work of other artists. Discussing Picasso in his interview with Edward Lucie-Smith, for example, O'Hara says: "Picasso is passing by the Bateau-Lavoir and Picasso calls up and says, 'Max, come out.' And he says, 'I won't.' He says, 'Why won't you?' And he says, 'Because I'm in search of a style.' And Picasso walks down the hill and, as Max Jacob pulls his head back, says, 'There is no style.' That is the sort of thing that is, you know, like living and interesting" (*SS*, 13). To define how O'Hara understands Picasso's remark, "There is no style," we can turn to O'Hara's monograph on Pollock, where, as in the Picasso anecdote, we have two kinds of painters—one that is interested in a single style and one that is not, with the latter being, in O'Hara's view, the more interesting, accomplished artist. He writes: "Unlike his European contemporaries, art for him [i.e., Picasso] was not a matter of deciding upon a style and then exploring its possibilities. He explored the possibilities for discovery in himself as an artist, and in doing so he embraced, absorbed, and expanded all the material which he instinctively reached for, and which we later find to be completely pertinent to the work" (*AC*, 13). According to O'Hara, Pollock, like Picasso, does not commit himself to an individual style but to his materials. What holds Pollock's styles together is not so much the formal elements of the paintings as it is the individual artist himself. O'Hara writes: "If there is unity in the total oeuvre of Pollock, it is formed by a drastic self-knowledge which permeates each of his periods and underlies each change of interest, each search. In considering his work as a whole one finds the ego totally absorbed in the work" (*AC*, 13). This notion that the artist's personal involvement in the materials of his work is what unifies his work rather than the formal elements of the paintings themselves (even if the paintings might share some "family resemblances," as O'Hara says with respect to the work of Paul Klee), is stated on numerous occasions with respect to the work of artists such as Larry Rivers (1923–2002), Grace Hartigan (b. 1922), Jane Freilicher (b. 1924), and various others. This is what O'Hara means when he states later in his interview with Lucie-Smith that the artist should "be" the work himself (*SS*, 17).[33]

As Pepe Karmel has noted, this notion of being committed to one's materials is not a new concept with either Picasso or Pollock, as O'Hara sometimes implies. It was, in fact, a central tenet in the work of the art theorist Bernard Bosanquet (1828–1923) and in Gottfried

Semper's influential *Style in the Technical and Constructive Arts, or Practical Aesthetics* (1860), the latter being the theoretical basis for Gerhard Munthe's series of Norse legend tapestries and Piet Mondrian's geometrical paintings.[34] What is of particular importance in O'Hara's comments on Picasso and Pollock, however, is that this absence of a predetermined style of painting and a high degree of individual innovation—or, if not innovation, at least "unselfconscious" borrowing—are two of the minimal criteria of great art.

This presupposition underlies much of his critical evaluation of artists in his reviews for *ArtNews* between 1953 and 1955. O'Hara praises Juan Gris (1887–1927), for example, as one of "the great individualists of the [cubist] movement" and writes that "it seems that he would have painted the way he did whether there had been a movement or not."[35] He praises Grace Hartigan (then George Hartigan) for her highly individual paintings, which "seem to be a means of dealing with experience on her own terms and insisting on her own meanings."[36] In contrast, when he compares the work of three more or less unknown sculptors—Robert Cronbach, Elliott Sandow, and Jules Struppeck—O'Hara finds that while Struppeck is not more original than either Cronbach or Sandow, whose sculptures he dismisses as "too built" and "not yet art," Struppeck is "more generous in . . . feeling," which, he implies, makes his work somewhat closer to that of real art than the work of either Cronbach or Sandow.[37] The implication is that both Cronbach and Sandow are committed to a particular style while Struppeck is at least committed to exploring his feelings in his materials, even if he does not discover new or original forms in this process of exploration. In his review of Bennett Bradbury (1914–91), O'Hara dismisses Bradbury's commitment to one style as merely boring. He writes, for example, that his paintings "are academic; uniformity of execution and similarity of composition make it possible for him to maintain the same level throughout the show, but it is rather like looking at just one picture."[38]

This dialectic of "style" versus "no style" is nowhere clearer than in a review of the work of Miles Forst (b. 1923), in which O'Hara describes Forst's work in terms that could be applied to his own poems:

> Miles Forst does not believe that there is a "way" of good painting or that there can be a systematized personal projection. His work depends upon power and speed of performance, clarity and instantaneousness of perception. . . . He is more interested in experience than esthetics, and can use other people's work, with freedom and confidence, since they are what he

> is experiencing. The large collage, *Henry VIII*, for instance, starts from a brutal conception of one of Motherwell's most elegant periods, but the influence of Motherwell as one feels it in the picture is no more important than any other material of the collage; similarly, in the newspaper sketches a likeness to the telephone book sketches of Kline is immediately recognized, but one feels it to be accidental, as natural as an American poem which refers to the Chrysler Building. Forst is original in the inclusiveness of his work, which has an irony, a tang, all its own.[39]

Given this understanding that there can be no "*systematized* personal projection" (emphasis added) in great works of art, it is no surprise that O'Hara regards with disdain such systematizing efforts, a disdain clear from the parodic nature of "Personism," as well as a mock manifesto written with Rivers entitled "How to Progress in the Arts" (1959). More than the common artistic reluctance to explain one's work, O'Hara's unwillingness to comment on his work is rooted in this notion that in the exploration of the material of his craft the artist creates a style that is both personal and temporal. What unifies the work of the artist as a whole is the complex and, indeed, ever-changing self of the artist rather than a predetermined style common to all the individual works.

The Poetics of Saying "I"

For O'Hara, artistic creation is an act of passionate exploration of the poet's experience in the material of his medium rather than the "mechanical" enumeration of the alphabet of the mind. Furthermore, while O'Hara sees the completed works of art as symbols of the creative power that produces them, he seems to understand the end of art less in terms of taking us "closer" to this power and more in terms of enriching our experience of the material world. Art, in this sense, is like a sewage plant. It processes the poet's feelings as he interacts with the material world to create material objects that produce new objects of experience out of the old. Thus, while, for O'Hara, the completed work of art is an autonomous artifact, it is nevertheless related to the material world out of which it sprang, and, therefore, is more than just an instance of the mere play of empty signifiers. His own poems, O'Hara writes, create forms that, on the one hand, render simple phenomena more complex and, therefore, more interesting, and, on the other, render complex, "nebulous" phenomena more definite and concrete and, therefore, more immediate.

While O'Hara is part of the Anglo-American lyric tradition, he differs from other lyric poets in his understanding of the relationship between self-expression in art and self-knowledge. O'Hara understands the self to be an expression of the same power that is at work in the material world, but he does not hold that the exploration of the self in art somehow provides us with an image of a coherent and continuous self. While the self is a nexus of finite moments of feeling for O'Hara, he does not hope to somehow salvage some continuous or essential self out of these finite moments. These feelings are irreducible. However, he does understand poetry to be a "testament" of the self, in the sense that feelings are an expression of the power that holds the self together over a period of time. Thus, the self, for O'Hara, is both singular and multiple. In this sense, O'Hara differs from later so-called materialist poets such as Charles Bernstein (b. 1940) and Ron Silliman (b. 1947), who reject the notion of selfhood as a delusion and view the "voice" of the poem as nothing but a construct. O'Hara does not reject the notion of "voice," but rather remarks in "Homosexuality" (1954), "It is the law of my own voice I shall investigate" (*CP*, 182). What he however, is not some "ground" of the self, but rather that our feelings, our experience of the material world, cannot be reduced to a ground, but are themselves the irreducible building blocks of what we call the self.

2

Second Avenue

SECOND AVENUE IS ONE OF O'HARA'S MOST IMPORTANT LONG POEMS. In 1953, it was his longest poem to date and his most sustained exploration of the expressive limits of language. It is a sprawling amalgam of absurd images, disconnected phrases and quotation, newspaper clippings, short dramatic scenes, anecdotes, gossip, and literary and artistic references. O'Hara worked on the poem over a period of two months in spring 1953, writing most of it in between poses in Larry Rivers's garden studio overlooking the avenue itself as Rivers sculpted (*CP*, 529). Kenneth Koch explains that O'Hara had read an early draft of Koch's poem *When the Sun Tries to Go On* (1953) and that O'Hara had encouraged him to continue adding to it for as long as he could. Koch discovered that O'Hara began what was to become *Second Avenue* shortly after. A friendly competition ensued, with each sharing his daily results over the phone or lunch.[1]

Despite its length and radical linguistic innovations, *Second Avenue* is often dismissed as a mere experiment in "straight" surrealism, valuable only to the extent that it led to a breakthrough in poetic form.[2] Such an approach to the poem, however, is problematic. For one thing, it is incorrect to dismiss *Second Avenue* as an early experiment in poetic language and form. The linguistic inventiveness of the poem—O'Hara's surprising and illogical turns of phrases, dazzling metaphors, and absurd word combinations—can be seen in a great number of O'Hara's poems throughout his life. For example, poems such as "Oranges" (1949), "Easter" (1952), "In Memory of My Feelings" (1956), "Ode to Michael Goldberg ('s Birth and Other Births)" (1957) and "Biotherm (For Bill Berkson)" (1962) contain numerous absurd images and fragmented sentences and phrases, while a number of later poems, such as "F.O.I (A Vision of Westminster Abbey)" (1961), are even more indeterminate than *Second Avenue*. Furthermore, while O'Hara's later poems are, for the most part, more concrete, some examples of his direct, matter-of-fact "I do this I do that" poems can be found as early as 1950. In "Poem (Although I am a half hour)" (1950), for example, O'Hara begins by placing the poem and the poet at a specific time and place, and recounts what he thinks and what he does in simple diction and conversational tone. These are essential aspects of later "I do this I do that" poems, such as "A Step Away from Them" (1956) and "The Day Lady Died" (1956). Thus, the supposed shift in O'Hara's work from the more obscure language of *Second Avenue* to the more concrete language of these later poems cannot be described as a "breakthrough."

Added to this is the fact that *Second Avenue* was one of O'Hara's favorite poems throughout his life. In 1956, in a letter to Barney Rosset, editor of Grove Press, he communicates his love of the poem and expresses his desire that if not all, then at least part, of the poem be included in the then forthcoming *Meditations in an Emergency* (1957).[3] While Rosset did not include the poem in the volume, O'Hara himself arranged to have it published as a chapbook in 1960 with Totem Press. O'Hara's attitude toward the poem implies that he himself did not understand it to be part of an earlier, formative style, and while, as we shall see at the end of chapter, the poem has some clear shortcomings, the notion that *Second Avenue* is a mere experiment in plotting "a not-yet-existent tradition" is a rather simplified account of its place in O'Hara's work as a whole.

Perhaps more importantly, however, it is reductive to conceive of *Second Avenue* as an effort to write a "straight" surrealist work. This glosses over O'Hara's complex relationship to surrealism and hides a number of other important sources of the poem's style—in particular, the influence of Pasternak. While O'Hara never denied the influence of surrealism, he never claimed Breton or the surrealists as a direct influence on his work, either. Rather, as David LeHardy Sweet notes, he tended to speak of his love of French poets in general, and, in a letter to Kenneth Koch, equated surrealism with "modern French poetry as a whole."[4]

Instead of a means of accessing a so-called surrealty, automatism, for O'Hara, is an example of the aesthetic potential of the individual freedom or "openness" of the artist, and it is not a political or philosophical tool, as it is for Breton. In examining the influence of surrealism on Jackson Pollock, O'Hara states:

> The basic theory of Surrealism is a far greater liberation from the restrictions of preconceived form than any amount of idiosyncratic experimentation, and it finally destroyed the post-Renaissance vision of visual structure

> supported by the rationalizations and syllogisms of semi-popular science. That the principles of Surrealism were often expounded in painting by means perversely counter to the genuine accomplishment of Cubism does not negate the fact that Surrealism destroyed, where Cubism only undermined on the same rationalistic basis as before. Cubism was an innovation, Surrealism an evolution. The former dealt with technique, the latter with content. . . . Surrealism enjoined the duty, along with the liberation, of saying what you mean and meaning what you say, above and beyond any fondness for saying or meaning. (*AC*, 17–18)

While O'Hara struggles with the notion of freedom in his poems, it most often means an individual's immediate response to his or her present circumstances. Thus, it is not a surprise that artistic freedom is defined as the artist's immediate response to his or her materials and thus entails the dutiful rejection of "preconceived forms" and the breaking of artistic rules.[5] While cubism broke the rules of style—of how art represented the visual world—surrealism broke with the rationalistic basis of art itself. While O'Hara acknowledges that the freedom surrealism offers (and that he himself desires) is also a prescriptive one (it is, after all, a "duty"), it is nevertheless one that provides the artist with more creative possibilities than other theories of artistic creation—in particular, what O'Hara calls the "post-Renaissance vision of visual structure supported by the rationalizations and syllogisms of semi-popular science." Here, O'Hara seems to be referring to the traditional use of perspective in painting to re-create what was thought to be the "real" visual structure of the world. While Braque and Picasso's early cubist paintings were the first works of art to call into question this understanding of the visual structure of the world, the paintings themselves were still preoccupied with objects of visual experience, and it was not until surrealism and abstract expressionism that the source material of artistic creation was something other than visual experience. There is also a sense, however, in which the freedom that surrealism offers is not from rules and content alone, but from reason—which, for O'Hara, is defined as prose hypotaxis, or what he calls the "syllogisms of semi-popular science."

O'Hara's understanding here of surrealism as an example of the aesthetic value of freedom from logic and the "restrictions of preconceived form" and content is a version of surrealism that was common among American artist in New York long before O'Hara wrote either *Second Avenue* or his monograph on Jackson Pollock. In his excellent study on the influence of surrealism on American painting in the

1940s, Jeffrey Wechsler traces the influence of automatism on American painters from Breton and Salvador Dali (1904–89) to Gerome Kamrowski (1914–2004), William Baziotes (1912–63), and Pollock.[6] While these painters, Wechsler notes, were interested in automatism as a method of composition, they rejected its more radical political implications and philosophical foundations, applying it rather, with typical American pragmatism, "directly toward the problem of picture-making."[7]

This American recasting of automatism as a technical tool in the creation of paintings is most evident in a paper that Robert Motherwell wrote for the exposition "The First Papers in Surrealism" at the Whitelaw-Reid Mansion in 1942, which included the work of Motherwell himself, as well as that of Baziotes, Pollock, Kamrowski, and Peter Busa (1914–85).[8] Robert Hobbs writes that Motherwell formulates here what would later become a tenet of so-called abstract expressionist art:

> [T]he Abstract Expressionists did not envision the unconscious as a potential conduit to a no-longer-accessible realm defined as "the marvelous," as Matta's description suggests. For them, its chief characteristic was its amorphous potential, which was not at all understandable until it became immanent. The initial and necessary translation of this amorphous content works to the advantage of the unconscious since it preserves its distinct otherness while spontaneity and pentimenti (layering), which became the group's trademarks, are signs of their improvisational way of working, reinforcing the contingency that attends the unconscious' conversion to an artistic medium.[9]

In other words, Motherwell's "plastic automatism" is a means of picture making, whose principal purpose is not to discover some "absolute reality" but to harness the "amorphous potential" of the unconscious for pictorial effect.

When O'Hara writes in his monograph on Pollock that surrealism provided "a far greater liberation from the restrictions of preconceived form," it is, it seems, Motherwell's version of surrealism to which he is referring (*AC*, 17). His understanding, furthermore, that Pollock's "insight" in his work is the result of "the accumulation of decisions along the way and the eradication of conflicting beliefs" is evocative of Motherwell's definition of art as the product of an individual consciousness (*AC*, 25). Thus, like numerous artists before him, O'Hara maintains a place for personal choice, however predetermined or limited, in his poetics. O'Hara's numerous references in his criticism to the "achievement" and "perceptions" of a particular artist—be it Willem de Kooning's in "Nature and New Painting" (1954), Pasternak's in "About Zhivago and His Poems" (1959), or his above remark with respect to Jackson Pollock—show that, for O'Hara, like Motherwell, one of the minimum requirements of art is that it be shaped, to some degree, by the conscious intervention of the artist. Hence, as he writes in "A Terrestrial Cuckoo" (1951), the act of writing is not pure intuition, or pure expression, but an "intuitive craft" (*CP*, 62).

While *Second Avenue* was written six years before O'Hara's monograph on Jackson Pollock, there is nothing in O'Hara's criticism or poems to suggest that he moved from an espousal of "straight" surrealism in *Second Avenue* to a more nuanced and up-to-date version. In addition to the fact that O'Hara rejected the philosophical and political idealism of surrealism in his poem "Memorial Day 1950," it is important to note that after O'Hara moved to New York in 1951, he immersed himself in the lives and work of artists such as Joan Mitchell (1925–92), Helen Frankenthaler (b. 1928), Nell Blaine (1922–96), Grace Hartigan, Jane Freilicher, and Larry Rivers, as well as poets such as Ashbery, Koch, and Barbara Guest (1920–2006), among others. The initial contact with the New York art world took place at the Cedar Tavern at the corner of University Place and Eighth Street, where the artists would gather after a day of isolation in their respective studios. O'Hara writes: "The milieu of those days, and it's funny to think of them in such a way since they are so recent, seems odd now. We were all in our early twenties. John Ashbery, Barbara Guest, Kenneth Koch and I, being poets, divided our time between the literary bar, the San Remo, and the artist's bar, the Cedar Tavern. In the San Remo we argued and gossiped; in the Cedar we often wrote poems while listening to the painters argue and gossip" (*CP*, 512).

In addition to frequenting the Cedar and the San Remo, however, soon O'Hara would often visit the artists' studios during the day. Because of this, in his first year in New York he appeared in five paintings—three by Nell Blaine, one by Larry Rivers, and one by Grace Hartigan. Freliecher explains that O'Hara "used to just love to be around the studio and he would come and help me stretch my canvases, which was like a great privilege to him," and Rivers explains that O'Hara "was a professional fan."[10] At the rather late date of 1953, two years after O'Hara had moved to New York, at a time when he had been invited to give a second talk at The Club, and shortly before he would begin work as a reviewer for *ArtNews*, it is unlikely that he was trying his hand at "straight" surrealism in a poem such as *Second Avenue.*

Rather than a mere experiment in surrealism, *Second Avenue* is a poem in which O'Hara, indebted to Boris Pasternak's notion of art as an expression of the energy of life itself and Robert Motherwell's notion of "plastic automatism," explores the coming into being of conscious experience and shows the flow of experience. In the process of his exploration, furthermore, the poet expands language's expressive possibilities, through which our experience of the world is, in part, mediated. In this sense, the poem could be understood as an exploration of the potential value of language and of present experience as a sort of existential argument against the need to posit an extraexperiential telos that organizes and gives meaning to present experience.

Second Avenue

The poem is written in the first-person singular and is addressed to an unidentified "you." The representational content of the poem is, for the most part, obscure. While the title of the poem is *Second Avenue*, there are few recognizable images of New York City or references to city life. Furthermore, while there is a semblance of narrative relation between the eleven sections of the poem, the poem is, in the end, disjunctive and disconnected.

The first section of the poem begins with an allusion to John Milton's "L'Allegro" (1633). O'Hara writes:

> Quips and players, seeming to vend astringency off-hours,
> celebrate diced excesses and sardonics, mixing pleasures,
> as if proximity were staring at the margin of a plea. . . .
>
> (*CP*, 139)

The noun "quip" is, of course, a witty or sarcastic remark. O'Hara uses it in this case, however, to refer to people who are "jokers" or "jesters"; and, in this sense, the phrase "Quips and players" recalls Milton's "Quips and Cranks" in "L'Allegro."[11] The rest of the opening lines confirm this allusion. While O'Hara's "Quips and players" "vend astringency off-hours," Milton's "Quips and Cranks" possess "wanton Wiles."[12] Furthermore, while Milton writes of living in "unreprovèd pleasures free," O'Hara writes of celebrating "diced excesses and sardonics, mixing pleasure."[13] And while there are "wreathèd

Smiles" in Milton, which implies that there is something not quite right about these "unreprovèd pleasures," there is also something abnormal about the "excesses" and "pleasures" in *Second Avenue*, sold by jokers and jesters "off-hours."[14]

The opening section of *Second Avenue* is also evocative of Hart Crane's "Moment Fugue" (1926).[15] In "Moment Fugue," Crane describes a "syphillitic [*sic*] selling violets calmly / and daisies" and "hyacinths," which has certain similarities to O'Hara's outcast quips and players selling "astringency off-hours."[16] However, while in "Moment Fugue" the eyes of the "syphillitic" fall "mute and sudden (dealing change / for lilies) / Beyond the roses that no flesh can pass," O'Hara's "I" bursts forth in what seems to be an effort to avoid silence at all costs.

Rather than exploring these strange pleasures or expanding on these allusions to Milton or Crane, O'Hara leaves both, only returning to Crane at the end of the poem. However, these first three lines do set up a comparison to lines 4–13 that follow, to which O'Hara returns later in the poem. In these lines, O'Hara shifts his attention, as he states in his "Notes on *Second Avenue*" (1953), to logic. Referring to lines 5–13 of the opening section, O'Hara writes in his "Notes": "To put it very gently, I have a feeling that the philosophical reduction of reality to a dealable-with system so distorts life that one's 'reward' for this endeavor (a minor one, at that) is illness both from the inside and outside" (*CP*, 495). As it was for the surrealists, both European and American, reason is a sort of disease for O'Hara because it excludes the irrational and contingent elements of human existence that he sometimes associates with "life." Thus, the first three lines of the poem on "sardonics" and "mixing pleasures" can be contrasted with the "philosophical reduction of reality" in lines 4–13.

While O'Hara returns to this comparison of "sardonics" and "mixing pleasures" and the "philosophical reduction of reality" later in the poem, rather than contrasting "sardonics" with this "philosophical reduction of reality" in more detail in the lines that follow, line 14 marks a shift of both subject matter and tone. The poet addresses an unidentified "you," who, throughout the rest of the section, is presented as both antagonistic and ambivalent toward an "I" that is both insecure and confident, and which, at least in the first section, is the "I" of the poet. The section is peppered with images of sex, violence, and filth in what is, perhaps, a much more obscure representation of O'Hara's artistic coming-of-age recounted in "Memorial Day 1950." The final words of the section, "But now I have a larger following," seem to point to the poet emerging triumphant out of the jungle of critics and aesthetic trial and error (*CP*, 140). However, as is clear from sections 2 and 3, this sense of triumph is temporal, both repudiated ("My spirit is clouded") and reasserted ("I lead you to a stream which will lick you like a wasp") later in the poem (*CP*, 142).

In the second section, rather than expanding on the poet's nascent aesthetic, the poem shifts again. The section begins with the surprising line "What spanking opossums of sneaks are caressing the routes!" which seems to be intended to shock, as well as to break the rough thematic coherence of the first section (*CP*, 140). O'Hara addresses his poetics in the third line, stating, "I can only enumerate the somber instances of wetness," and asks in the fourth, "Is it a triumph?" He thus returns to the note of artistic triumph struck at the end of the first section. The rest of the second section is not devoted to enumerating "instances of wetness," or to reflecting on the poet's artistic triumphs, but to exploring images of light and motion. Here, the poet addresses himself as a "you" that accepts the "poisonous sting of the spine," the "golden efflorescence of nature" that, in turn, blossoms as a tree. The poet looks to the sky and sees "an animal kingdom of jealousy in parachutes / descending upon the highway," which, in turn, evokes an image of "open fields" in the poet's mind. These images are faintly resonant of the cubist and futurist understanding of art as, among other things, an expression of energy akin to light and motion, but, perhaps, with more references to nature (trees, clouds and fields) than are found in the work of Apollinaire or Marinetti, for example. O'Hara ends this much shorter section with one final reference to the first section of the poem. Evoking the "diced excesses" of the opening lines of the poem, he writes:

> Dice! into the lump and crush of archness and token angels
> you burn your secret preferment and ancient streaming,
>
> as a gasp of laughter at desire, and disorder, and dying.
>
> (*CP*, 141)

Here, the rejected "philosophical reduction of reality" in the opening section is presented as "a gasp of laughter at desire, and disorder, and dying" and is contrasted with the image of dice, which evokes the notion of chance.

At the beginning of the third section, O'Hara shifts his attention again. Picking up on the tangential phrase "token angels" at the end of the second section, he explores what he calls "the science of legendary elegies" (*CP*, 141). The section is devoted to the religious images of "Blue negroes" who resemble "priests . . . in their bedrooms at dawn," "Mayan idols," "circumcision of a black horse," "drunken Magi," and "Apollo" (*CP*, 141–42). At the end of the section, O'Hara turns from these religious images and addresses the "you" of the poem, which is both the "you" of the reader and, perhaps, the "you" of the first section of the poem:

> so you are silent, aren't you? Well, I shall be older
> and uglier than you, and my least motion shall wither
> the vertiginous breath which is earth meeting sky meeting sea,
> as in the legend of a sovereign who did and who was.
> Immense flapping. I hold all of night in my one eye. You.
>
> (*CP*, 142)

The final religious image of this section is the image of the artist as God, who like the Son of God in Revelation 4:8 is praised by a host of angels, singing "Holy, holy, holy is the Lord God Almighty, who was, and is, and is to come." What makes the poet a "sovereign," however, is the fact that he, like the "I" of Whitman's *Song of Myself* (1891), contains "multitudes."[17] The word "eye" in this final line is a pun on "I"; thus, the poet holds "all of night" and all of "You" in his "I" or self. O'Hara thereby reverses both the biblical trope of God as light, and, it is interesting to note, the artistic trope, as expressed in Apollinaire's *The Cubist Painters*, of the work of art as a representation of light.

In the fourth and shortest section of the poem—a mere seven lines—O'Hara addresses the reader: "Is your throat dry with the deviousness of following? / I lead you to a stream which will lick you like a wasp" (*CP*, 142). While these lines raise the question of the obscure language of the poem, O'Hara does not maintain this "metanarrative" position, but rather returns to the sexual images of the first section, figuring the "you" of the poem reclining on "boards of starry nudging, / sisters of bar-girls in the haunches of the Himalayas." He ends the section with the question: "Or are you altitudes?" This, in turn, evokes Whitman's "multitudes," alluded to at the end of the third section (*CP*, 142).

The first four sections, therefore, are disparate and lacking in a coherent subject matter or theme, but they nevertheless contain several recurring images and thematic fragments. Images of sex, mythology, and the bizarre (such as "toothpaste falling on guitar strings"), staples of surrealistic art, are scattered throughout the first four sections, as the poet speaks in an all-inclusive "I," addressing an instable "you" that is at times both antagonistic and passive as the poet reflects on, among numerous other things, artistic creation itself. In fact, if O'Hara had stopped the poem at the end of section 4—and one wonders if he had, in fact, considered stopping here, given the shortness of the section, the metanarrative position he assumes, and the poetic turn in the first line of the section—Perloff and Ashbery would have been more correct in identifying at least the style of the poem itself in terms of conventional surrealism.

The fifth section of the poem, however, marks a major shift. While in the first four sections of the poem, O'Hara explores the language of the unfolding conscious experience, in the fifth section O'Hara begins to include language from other sources, ranging from anecdotes and fictional stories to parodies of rational argumentation and newspaper clippings. Because of this, the fifth section and the sections that follow become both more comprehensible and more obscure. While individual passages of some of section 5 and of the sections that follow are often clear enough as self-contained units, in the context of the respective sections it is, in fact, much more difficult to extract a theme for the sections because of these passages that seem to be dropped into the poem at random.

The fifth section begins with the same sexually charged dialectic of the "I" and the "you" of the first four sections, where the "you" becomes an object of desire of the "I" of the poem ("You are lean, achieved, ravished, acute, light, tan, / waving, stolen, lissome in whispering, salivary in intent). However, O'Hara shifts his attention to his personal life and writes in a conversational tone and in a simple, if abbreviated, prose:

> I met Joe, his hair pale as the eyes of fields of maize
> in August, at the gallery, he said you're the first Creon
> of 1953, congrats. Your costume, he said, was hand
> over fist. If you worked harder you could remake
> old Barrymore movies, you're that statuesque, he said.
>
> (*CP*, 143)

After this brief anecdote, O'Hara returns to the disconnected, dense, and absurd language that characterized the first four sections, writing: "For when the window, the ice in it, ran, the fish leaped forth / and returned where they wished to return to and from" (*CP*, 143). This is followed, however, by the beginning of what seems to be a rape scene and at least one further anecdote. The section, then, ends with a long parody of logical argumentation, which itself, in turn, includes another fictional scene—which O'Hara himself identifies in his "Notes on *Second Avenue*" as the beginning of a western—and more anecdotes and quotations from the poet's personal life, as well as an allusion to the romanticized relationship of Verlaine and Rimbaud (*CP*, 144).

In the following sections, the poem returns again to images of artistic creation, anecdotes, newspaper clippings, and further references to artists and poets. In the eleventh and final section of the poem, however, O'Hara writes in the first person and returns to the tone and diction of the first four sections. He begins the section with a reference to the sculpture that Rivers is making of him, reveling perhaps in the concrete example of what is one of O'Hara's favorite tropes—that of the artist himself as a work of art. He writes:

> My hands are Massimo Plaster, called "White Pin in the Arm of the Sea"
> and I'm blazoned and scorch like a fleet of windbells down the Pulaski Skyway
> tabletops of Vienna carrying their bundles of cellophane to the laundry,
> ear to the tongue, glistening semester of ardency, young-old daringnesses
> at the foot of the most substantial art product of our times
>
> (*CP*, 150)

O'Hara's focus on the hands of the statue, rather than on other more common centers of attention such as the head or the face, begins what is a double description in this final section of both Rivers's actual statue and O'Hara's work, figured in the statue itself. The hands, as the physical means of artistic creation for both the artist and the poet, are called here the "White Pin in the Arm of the Sea," which recalls the "distinction" of the poet described in the first section as "a quill at the bottom of the sea." Here the beauty of the poet's hands, and, in turn, his art, is lost on most people, who are, both literally and figuratively, looking elsewhere. The statue is "blazoned" and scorched, symbolizing, perhaps, the poet himself, whose "wounds" become a sort of flute (here "windbells") as he flies in the "Pulaski Skyway." The statue, in which both O'Hara's actual body and his body of work are figured, is pronounced with some tongue-in-cheek the "most substantial art product of our times."

However, this "substantial art product"—both Rivers's statue and O'Hara's work—is not recognized in the artists' home country. It flies in the air like an airplane and arrives in Mexico, "the palace of stammering sinking success" (*CP*, 150). O'Hara writes:

> O paradise! my airplanes known as "Banana Line Incorporealidad,"
> saviors of connections and spit, dial HYacinth 9–9945, "Isn't that
> a conundrum?" asked him Sydney Burger, humming "Mein Yiddisher Mama"
> I emulate the black which is a cry but is not voluptuary like a warning,
> which has lines, cuts, drips, aspirates, trembles with horror
>
> (*CP*, 150)

O'Hara associates blackness in this final section of *Second Avenue* with both horror and sex. O'Hara writes, for example, of "black looks at the base of the spine!" and "kisses on the medulla oblongata / of an inky clarity!" (*CP*, 150).

Rather than exploring this motif of darkness in further detail, however, O'Hara returns to Rivers's statue:

> Elbow of roaches! You wear my white rooster like guerdon in vales
> of Pompeian desires, before utter languorousness puts down its chisel,"
> and the desert is here. "You've reached the enormous summit of passion
> which is immobility forging an entrail from the pure obstruction of the air.
>
> (*CP*, 150)

Rivers has completed his work ("utter languorousness puts down its chisel"), which is experienced as both a moment of dejection ("and the desert is here") and exuberant triumph ("You've reached the enormous summit of passion"), as O'Hara completes his poem as well.

The syntactic and structural dislocation and disjunction of *Second Avenue* serves a number of ends. First, these elements express what O'Hara perceives to be the nature of experience. Events happen. One perception of the mind follows another. The previous experience does not have a discursive relationship to the next, nor does each perception or experience relate to the overall meaning of our life, because, for O'Hara, our experience has no meaning outside of itself. While all our experiences constitute who we are, we do not, nor can we, rationalize them in some harmonious narrative. Rather, each moment should be felt in the present for whatever it is, and valued for the sensations it produces.

That life, for O'Hara, has no continuous pattern in the sense that there is no constant extraexperiential telos that orders and gives meaning to our experience is clear from remarks he made in his journal in

1949. He writes: "Mary McCarthy says 'the most harrowing experience of man' is 'the failure to feel steadily, to be able to compose a continuous pattern'; but if one does feel steadily and the pattern is horrific? . . . I feel steadily but there is no pattern, there can be no pattern, there is only being; you cannot sell yourself, you cannot stand that far apart from your self to dicker, if there is any integrity in you" (*EW*, 109–10). The comment by McCarthy that " 'the most harrowing experience of man' is 'the failure to feel steadily' " is from her essay on Laurence Olivier's *Hamlet* in the *Partisan Review*, where, in examining the character of Hamlet, she writes: "Sir Laurence Olivier's is the only *Hamlet* which seizes this inconsecutiveness and makes of it an image of suffering, of the failure to feel steadily, to be able to compose a continuous pattern, which is the most harrowing experience of man. Hamlet, a puzzle to himself, is seen by Olivier as a boy, whose immaturity is both his grace and his frailty."[18] For O'Hara, however, "this inconsecutiveness," as McCarthy calls it, is not due to a "failure to feel steadily." Rather, it is what he feels to be the structure of feeling itself. Feeling, for him, has no inherent pattern, and no "continuous pattern" can be composed from it; because in order to do so one must assume a position outside of one's own experience, which is impossible.

Second, the syntax and structure prevent the reader from reducing the meaning of the poem to individual words or controlling "deep" images or metaphors. O'Hara's use of logical qualifiers and conjunctions both to create an expectation of correlation and, and the same time, to prevent such correlation thwarts all efforts of locating the meaning of the poem at the level of the image or phrase itself. As he does throughout the poem, O'Hara avoids the use of periods, and uses commas (where it would be more correct to use periods) as a means of adding new, and often unrelated, images to previous ones. He places exclamation points in relation to a particular word rather than in relation to a sentence, and uses logical markers to evoke and postpone, rather than provide, a sense of connectedness. He begins clauses without finishing them, or, if he does, he often finishes them with a non sequitur. The result is that it is impossible to hold either individual sections of the poem or the poem as a whole together as a unit of thought, or to assign some sort of essential meaning to particular references or metaphors.

Indeed, the most common function of allusion, as Gregory Machacek notes, is hermeneutic.[19] An allusion contributes to the meaning of a particular text, most often in either unlocking the meaning of the passage in which it appears or in nuancing what might otherwise be too simple a statement. In *Second Avenue*, however, O'Hara's allusions, in particular his learned references, do not tend to unlock the meaning of a particular passage, but rather most often place us in front of a reference that we are unable to make rational sense of in the context of the poem as a whole.

O'Hara's references to Milton's "L'Allegro" and Hart Crane in the first section of the poem and to the second coming of Christ in the third do not help us to understand the themes of the poem, but rather evoke and frustrate a search for meaning. In doing so, one could say that O'Hara represents our effort to reduce the meaning of his poems to a particular word or phrase, or allusion, an effort that functions as a metaphor for our search for meaning in life. O'Hara uses meaningless allusions to show that this search for meaning is misplaced and to focus our attention on the present moment of conscious experience. Instead of looking past our present experience to find some hidden "deep image" or posited teleological end in which all of our experience finds meaning, O'Hara hopes to focus our attention on the richness of conscious experience itself.

O'Hara discusses this use of allusion to represent the search for meaning in his short essay on Rivers's work, "Larry Rivers: *The Next to Last Confederate Soldier*" (1959). O'Hara notes, first of all, that the conversion of subject and object in abstract paintings, where the painting is the object itself of its own creation, forces us as viewers to associate the painting with another object for it to have meaning for us. In this sense, the artist no longer represents his meaning by using figures, which then function as metaphors, but forces us as viewers to produce the metaphors ourselves. It is in this sense that the artist can be said, according to O'Hara, to hold up "a mirror of color and/or impasto to the viewer," representing the viewer himself in his effort to associate the work of art with another object of perception, a particular feeling or emotion (*SS*, 96). Rivers, however, uses both recognizable images and abstract forms in his paintings; and while he seems to provide the meaning of his paintings in the images he produces, in the end he withholds his meaning in presenting these images in a context that prevent us from making sense of them. Unlike painters who recognize the audience and provide them with a mirror of themselves, "Rivers," O'Hara writes, both refuses "to recognize the audience" and denies "the audience the opportunity to recognize him" (*SS*, 96). While Rivers's refusal to recognize his audience in presenting them with images that cannot be scrutinized could be understood as catering to some form of coterie, O'Hara himself provides another explanation of Rivers's images. He writes: "*The Soldier's* fluctuation between figurative absence and abstract presence comes from an adamant attachment to substance, which is its source of energy. That is all, no identity. In his work Rivers is playing out, at whatever cost to himself, the drama of our lack" (*SS*, 96). Rivers's use of recognizable images, in other words, whose meanings in the respective works cannot be identified represents the "drama" of our failure to rationalize all of experience.

Third, the syntax and structure of the poem as critics such as Perloff, Smith, and Sweet have noted, make the tactile qualities of the words themselves much more evident. This is one of the principal strategies of the poem itself. When the words are detached from a recognizable discursive context, the material elements of the words—the visual and aural qualities of the words on the page—come to the fore. As O'Hara writes with respect to the work of Claes Oldenburg in 1963, in focusing our attention on the material nature of the subject matter of a work of art the artist causes us to become more aware of the tactile contrasts of present experience. O'Hara writes:

> Where most of the other artists grouped by opinion into the "new realists" or "pop art" movement tend to make their art *out of* vulgar (in the sense of everyday) objects, images and emblems, Oldenburg makes the very objects and symbols themselves, with the help of papier-mâché, cloth, wood, glue, paint and whatever other mysterious materials are inside and on them, *into* art. . . . With the perverse charms of Gulliver and of Alice-in-Wonderland, Oldenburg makes one feel almost hysterically present, alert, summoned to the party. There is no hint of mysticism, no "significance," no commentary, in the work. (*SS*, 141–42)

This attention to the materials of the work itself, which, in turn, makes us feel "present, alert," can be observed at the beginning of the eighth section of *Second Avenue*, where O'Hara writes:

> Candidly. The past, the sensations of the past. Now!
> in cuneiform, of umbrella satrap square-carts with hotdogs
> and onions of red syrup blended, of sand bejewelling the prepuce
> in tank suits, of Majestic Camera Stores and Schuster's,
> of Kenneth in an abandoned storeway on Sunday cutting ever more
> insinuating lobotomies of a yet-to-be-more-yielding world
> of ears, of a soprano rallying at night in a cadenza, Bill,
>
> (*CP*, 146)

While the words here are not "in cuneiform," the material elements of the words themselves are made more evident because of the fact that the passage lacks a clear discursive narrative. For example, the harsh sound produced by the alliteration of *s* in "satrap square-carts," coupled with the spondaic foot of "square-carts" contrasts with the smoother *s* sound and more fluid meter of "red syrup blended" and "sand bejewelling the prepuce" in the following line. This contrasting repetition of *s* continues throughout the rest of the passage as it fluctuates from its harsher sound in words such as "Majestic Camera Stores and Schuster's" and its smoother sound in "storeway" and "Sunday." This attention to the aural and visual elements of the words provides them with a certain tangible presence that is often lost or at least ignored when used in the context of the narrative prose sentence.

In addition to bringing the material elements of words to the fore, a fourth and often ignored aspect of dislocation and disjunction in *Second Avenue* is that these serve to expand our experiential knowledge of the material world in expanding the connotative possibilities of words themselves. O'Hara coins absurd metaphors, for example, in order to break out of our repetitive and narrow representations of experience, which, in turn, condition our interactions with the world. Finding new metaphors is part of O'Hara's effort to find new, exhilarating ways of representing our experience to ourselves and, therefore, a means of opening ourselves up to nuances or complexities of our existence that are ignored or undervalued.

In addition to using metaphors, O'Hara uses single recurring words to mean different, even antithetical things, and this expands the words' connotative meaning. For example, O'Hara refers to "ice" on six separate occasions: twice in section 1, twice in section 5, and once in each of sections 7 and 10. In addition to this, he refers to "my glacial immodesty" and a "lampooned frigid scalper" in section 1 and the "snowing snow" in section 7. The image of ice, however, does not have some sort of stable symbolic meaning. In the first section, O'Hara uses ice to evoke an image of dazzling flashes of light ("I scintillate like a glass of ice") and in the fifth section to evoke a sense of bizarre otherworldliness ("and ice / telephone wires! was knotted, spelling out farce"), while in the seventh and tenth sections, it has no particular significance at all (*CP*, 140, 144, 145, 149).

Another example is his use of the word "blue." While O'Hara uses the word "blue" in the third and seventh sections to evoke a sense of otherness, referring to "Blue negroes" and "stillborn blue brothers of / entirely other races," it is unclear what significance the color might have in the eighth section, where O'Hara refers to "the landscape / less blue than prehistorically," and the ninth section, where he writes of "yellow and blue" lumber and a "blue fire-escape" (*CP*, 141, 145, 146–47, 148). Green and orange, instead of blue, fire escapes appear in the tenth section of the poem, furthermore, with no apparent shift in significance (*CP*, 149). O'Hara uses white on six and yellow on four different occasions.

Fifth, the syntax and structure in *Second Avenue* levels the hierarchy implied in hypotaxis. While the English prose sentence distinguishes between things such as main clause and subordinate clause, and subject and object, and, therefore, creates a hierarchy between the words within the sentence, parataxis creates a situation where each word is potentially just as important, just as worthy of our attention, as the main subject and verb in a typical English prose sentence. In this sense, the poem proposes a more "egalitarian" sentence, where each word is of equal value. The use of illogical phrases and false syllogism is also an attempt to break down the hierarchy established in prose, and perhaps is a critique of rational discourse.

After *Second Avenue*

Therefore, rather than a mere experiment in surrealism, or a simplistic effort to "deconstruct" meaning, *Second Avenue* is a poem in which O'Hara explores his present experience and, in the process, works to renew both language itself and our experience of the material world that is, in part, mediated through it. O'Hara's use of meaningless allusions, parataxis, and absurd images and metaphors prevents us from reducing the meaning of the poem to one controlling image or symbol and becomes an enactment of the irreducible nature of experience. This lack of narrative and thematic structure removes words from their normal syntactical contexts and, therefore, focuses our attention on the material nature of words themselves. O'Hara's absurd metaphors and images function to expand language's connotative and expressive possibilities.

This understanding of the irreducible nature of experience implied in *Second Avenue* was one that was both a source of satisfaction and of dissatisfaction for O'Hara throughout his life, mitigated, as it was, by his awareness that experience is always temporal. In "Poem (And tomorrow morning at 8 o'clock in Springfield, Massachusetts)" (1956), reflecting on the recent death of his aunt, O'Hara writes:

> When I die, don't come, I wouldn't want a leaf
> to turn away from the sun—it loves it there.
> There's nothing so spiritual about being happy
> but you can't miss a day of it, because it doesn't last.
>
> (*CP*, 244)

The image of the leaf in the sun as a metaphor for our experience of the present moment in all its fullness is followed with the knowledge that "it doesn't last." For O'Hara, this is the great tragedy of human existence.

It is at this point, however, that O'Hara, comparing his aunt's life and his own, refigures his living in the present as a form of love for the present world. He writes:

> So this is the devil's dance? Well I was born to dance.
> It's a sacred duty, like being in love with an ape,
> and eventually I'll reach some great conclusion, like assumption,
> when at last I meet exhaustion in these flowers, go straight up.
>
> (*CP*, 244)

The "devil's dance" is O'Hara's lifestyle, which is, presumably, in stark contrast to the lifestyle of his aunt, who, O'Hara tells us earlier in the poem, is being buried in a convent. Yet, while O'Hara's life may seem devilish according to certain standards, he recasts it here as a "religious" commitment to living in the present. It is a "sacred duty" that will end when the poet dies and (as in the ascension of Christ) goes "straight up." Figuring living in the present as a "sacred duty"—which is, he notes, a form of love—is a means for O'Hara to transcend the tragedy of death. Though one could question whether or not this notion of love as something that is sacred and self-sacrificial (in the sense that it is an ethical obligation or"duty") contradicts O'Hara's otherwise hedonistic understanding of the meaning and value of experience. However, as will be shown in chapter 5, it is a notion of love that O'Hara espoused throughout his life, and one that provides an important balance to what might otherwise be decried as crass poetic solipsism.

3
Naming Things

> Maybe we're here only to say: *house*
> *bridge, well, gate, jug, olive tree, window—*
> at most, *pillar, tower* . . . but to say them, remember,
> oh, to say them in a way that the things themselves
> never dreamed of existing so intensely. When this silent
> earth urges lovers on, isn't it her secret reason
> to make everything shudder with ecstasy in them?
> Doorsill: how much it means to a pair of lovers
> to wear down the sill of their own
> door a little more, them too, after so many
> before them, and before all those to come . . . gently.
> (—Rainer Maria Rilke, "Ninth Elegy," *Duino Elegies)*

> I can't really tell
> that I'm alive, except
> I name the world.
> (—Frank O'Hara, "Four Little Elegies")

One of the most distinctive elements of O'Hara's work is his use of names and everyday nouns to write a poem. O'Hara's names, however, have proven difficult for the critic attempting to explain their poetic value. If O'Hara's use of language in poems such as *Second Avenue* is an effort, on the one hand, to show that "feelings are our facts," and, on the other, to "muddy" language, his straightforward use of names and nouns in his "I do this I do that" poems is a means of providing the "nebulous" forms of experience a more concrete if nevertheless temporary form. This, in turn, allows us to come into contact with the "contours" of our feeling by capturing the constant flow of conscious experience and is part of an effort to "stop" time itself, thus allowing us to experience time in its fullness rather than as a moment of loss. Following Paul Goodman's call in "Advance-Guard Writing, 1900–1950" for the poet to reestablish a "plausible" context for the expression of feeling, O'Hara names events and people to ground his "I do this I do that" poems in an actual occasion, which allows him to express an emotion or feeling that does not seem constructed or trite, but rather seems authentic.[1] In this sense, naming is an affirmation of the value of our experience of things and events in face of the seeming meaninglessness and boredom of life.

As Marjorie Perloff notes, the naming of things and events in O'Hara's work is something he learned, in part, from Williams (*FOH*, 25, 44–48). For Williams, naming is both a means of defining and of creating. In *Spring and All* (1923), for example, he writes: "Understood in a practical way, without calling upon mystic agencies, of this or that order, it is that life becomes actual only when it is identified with ourselves. When we name it, life exists."[2] To name is to define a moment of experience. When "we name" our perception, we give it a form, we give it a material existence in language. Hence, when "we name it, life exists." In his poems, Williams is concerned both with providing "new forms, new names for experience" and with arranging the words of his poem to produce a certain effect and to draw our attention to their status as words, and, therefore, to the poem's status as a construct rather than as a form of representation.[3]

What Williams names is, most often, an image or an instant of experience suspended in time. James E. B. Breslin remarks that while "Williams slows us down and concentrates our attention on both the object and the words representing it," O'Hara names to capture the "ever-changing" nature "of temporal process itself."[4] Rather than slow down and linger over his perception of things, which may lead him to reflect on the meaning of this experience, O'Hara moves from one experience to the next in his poems with few moments for pause. Rather than help us see the "kinaesthetic impact of the various forms" of a poem, as Peter Halter notes is the case in Williams's work, O'Hara names to establish an authentic context in which to express a moment of feeling and to provide the ever-changing flow of experience with a temporal form; and this, in turn, allows us to experience time as a moment of fullness rather than as a moment of loss.[5]

In "A Step Away from Them," O'Hara's naming re-creates the process of perception. It is a poem about the importance of feeling each temporal moment in its detail, and the value of art in sustaining our interest in life:

A STEP AWAY FROM THEM

It's my lunch hour, so I go
for a walk among the hum-colored
cabs. First, down the sidewalk

where laborers feed their dirty
glistening torsos sandwiches
and Coca-Cola, with yellow helmets
on. They protect them from falling
bricks, I guess. Then onto the
avenue where skirts are flipping
above heels and blow up over
grates. The sun is hot, but the
cabs stir up the air. I look
at bargains in wristwatches. There
are cats playing in sawdust.
On
to Times Square, where the sign
blows smoke over my head, and higher
the waterfall pours lightly. A
Negro stands in a doorway with a
toothpick, languorously agitating.
A blond chorus girl clicks: he
smiles and rubs his chin. Everything
suddenly honks: it is 12:40 of
a Thursday.
Neon in daylight is a
great pleasure, as Edwin Denby would
write, as are light bulbs in daylight.
I stop for a cheeseburger at JULIET'S
CORNER. Giulietta Masina, wife of
Federico Fellini, è bell' attrice.
And chocolate malted. A lady in
foxes on such a day puts her poodle
in a cab.
There are several Puerto
Ricans on the avenue today, which
makes it beautiful and warm. First
Bunny died, then John Latouche,
then Jackson Pollock. But is the
earth as full as life was full, of them?
And one has eaten and one walks,
past the magazines with nudes
and the posters for BULLFIGHT and
the Manhattan Storage Warehouse,
which they'll soon tear down. I
used to think they had the Armory
Show there.

A glass of papaya juice
and back to work. My heart is in my
pocket, it is Poems by Pierre Reverdy.

(CP, 257–58)

In "A Step Away from Them," O'Hara names what he sees and hears without pausing to reflect on the relationship between these perceptions, or the meaning of them in relation to his life, until the middle of the fourth section when he recalls the death of three friends: the poet V. R. Lang, the composer John Latouche, and Jackson Pollock. This recollection is both an elegiac moment and a moment of crisis. On the one hand, he elegizes the fullness with which each of his friends lived life. On the other hand, he questions whether experience itself is, as Breslin notes, a process "of loss and decline," and, related to this, whether the life that the earth contains is enough to counterbalance his sense of loss.[6]

In the first three and a half sections of the poem, O'Hara names his experience. He provides new, precise names for what he sees and hears. He names, for example, smaller units of experience. Rather than people, he sees "torsos" and "skirts . . . flipping above heels," he sees a "lady in / foxes" and "magazines with nudes." He disregards the distinction between established categories of perception in order to give his experience a form that is fresh and new. The cabs are not yellow but "hum-colored." The torsos are both "dirty" and "glistening." The "Negro" is both still and a center of attention or action, "languorously agitating" like the toothpick in his mouth. The "Puerto / Ricans," rather than the sun, make the street "beautiful and warm." He avoids stock phrases. "Everything," he writes at the end of the second section, "suddenly honks." "A lady in / foxes," he writes at the end of the third section, "on such a day puts her poodle / in a cab." To describe our experience in the same language and in same form dulls the sense of exhilaration we obtain from the meaning of the words. O'Hara wants to find new names and new forms for his experience in order to feel the animate nature of it in the words and phrases themselves.

However, part of the animate nature of our experience, for O'Hara, is its constant flow. There are no red wheelbarrows sitting in gardens in "A Step Away from Them." Everything is moving. The poet himself is walking "down the sidewalk" and in "Times Square," pausing only for some fast food—"a cheeseburger at JULIET'S / CORNER."

The "laborers" are eating, girls are walking, "cabs stir up the air," cats are "playing in sawdust," smoke is blowing over the poet's head, and a "waterfall pours lightly." A "chorus girl clicks" down the street.

We are not encouraged to linger over the names of the poem and find some symbolic meaning in them or find some principle that organizes both the selection and the order of objects of the poem. While O'Hara uses several metaphors in the poem, he also uses a fair number of proper names and simple adjectives, which modify simple nouns, all of which have no metaphorical meaning. He writes, for example, of "Coca-Cola," "Times Square," "Edwin Denby," "JULIET'S / CORNER," "Guilietta Masina," "Federico Fellini," "Puerto / Ricans," "BULLFIGHT," "the Manhattan Storage Warehouse," "the Armory / Show" and "Pierre Reverdy." In a number of instances, furthermore, he uses simple adjectival and adverbial phrases. He writes of "yellow helmets," "falling / bricks," "bargains in wristwatches," and "cats playing in sawdust," to give a few examples. These are all concrete, immediate descriptions of things, which do not offer much possibility of second or third meanings.

O'Hara organizes the narrative of the poem and uses simple sentences to further discourage us from reading more into the words of the poem than there is, as well as to move the poem forward at a certain speed. He uses simple conjunctions and prepositions of time and place, such as "and," "First," "then onto," and "On / to," and uses verbs that express the relationship between subject and object in as straightforward a way as possible. He uses, for example, verbs such as "be," "go," "look," and "stop," and "be" is used ten times. All of the verbs are in the present tense and express actions that are readily grasped. The relationship between the actions of the poem is that of a simple sequence, which is implied throughout the whole poem, but which O'Hara sometimes marks with the conjunction "then." O'Hara organizes the actions of the poem, it seems, in a form that prepares us for the next event of the poem, rather than focuses our attention on the details of his description of the events themselves. He organizes the poem as a whole so that, as Breslin writes, it seems to be "all forward push."[7] While O'Hara is indeed interested, as Williams is, in giving precise names to his experience, O'Hara also names to give the flow of his experience a set, albeit temporal, form, and this is unlike Williams. O'Hara's balancing of precision of perception and description of movement embodies a feeling of exhilaration and a preoccupation with the present.

The procession of objects and events of his lunch hour, however, comes to a sudden halt in the middle of the fourth section, when O'Hara remembers the recent death of three friends. For the first time in the poem, he reflects on, rather than describes, an event. As Breslin notes, the difficult wording of the rhetorical question is in stark contrast to the flow of the rest of the poem, and it forces us to pause to work out its multiple meanings.[8] On the one hand, O'Hara remembers the fullness of life that each of his friends possessed and questions whether the earth, where they are now buried, is as full as "life was full" of them. On the other hand, he questions whether the earth is as full of life now that they are gone. In this sense, he asks, as Breslin notes, whether "temporal experience is one of loss and decline."[9]

Related to this reflection on temporal experience is the painful realization that if one is to continue living an existence that is not plagued by the feeling of loss, one must cease to mourn the loss of, and perhaps even forget, deceased friends. While O'Hara steps "away from" those at his work at the beginning of the poem, he takes a more painful step "away from" his friends in the middle of the poem. O'Hara draws attention to this parallel in his repetition of the word "First." While the word expresses a sense of excitement when O'Hara uses it at the beginning of the poem to mark the first experience of what he hopes will be a refreshing break from the monotony of work, his use of it in the middle of the poem when he writes, "First / Bunny died, then John Latouche, / then Jackson Pollock," expresses a sense of despondency. After this moment of crisis and realization, the poet becomes detached from the world around him. The "I" becomes a "one" who continues to move and act, but who no longer feels the nuances and details of life as he did in the first three sections of the poem. He eats and "walks," but seems disinterested in what he eats and where he walks. Details, however, begin to come into focus, becoming less and less generic, from "magazines with nudes" to "posters for BULLFIGHT" to a specific building in a specific town, "the Manhattan Storage Warehouse," until the poet is again present as an "I" and involved in his experience of the world ("I used to think," he says of the warehouse, "they had the Armory / Show there").

Breslin writes that the crisis in "A Step Away from Them" is not resolved. It is "simply dropped." It is true that the poet does not answer his own question. Yet, the fact that he becomes interested in other things and is involved again in his experience suggests that, on this particular day, the earth is full of life enough to counterbalance his feeling of loss and that temporal experience is not one of loss and decline.

This is complicated, however, with O'Hara's reference to Pierre Reverdy (1889–1960) at the end of the poem. The meaning of this reference becomes clearer if we compare it to "Adieu to Norman, Bon Jour to Joan and Jean Paul" (1959), which O'Hara also ends with a reference to Reverdy. As he does in "A Step Away from Them," in "Adieu to Norman, Bon Jour to Joan and Jean Paul" O'Hara examines his current experience of the world and questions whether it is valuable enough in its own right to continue to see life as worth living. He comes to a somewhat darker conclusion, however, than he does in "A Step Away from Them." In the middle of the poem, he writes:

> the only thing to do is simply continue
> is that simple
> yes, it is simple because it is the only thing to do
> can you do it
> yes, you can because it is the only thing to do
>
> (*CP*, 329)

While to "continue," the poet reassures us, "is the only thing to do," the repeated questionings undermine our confidence in his affirmation. At the end of the poem, the doubts in the above lines, overpower his effort to hold them in check. He writes:

> and surely we shall not continue to be unhappy
> we shall be happy
> but we shall continue to be ourselves everything continues to be possible
> René Char, Pierre Reverdy, Samuel Beckett it is possible isn't it
> I love Reverdy for saying yes, though I don't believe it
>
> (*CP*, 329)

The conclusion of "Adieu to Norman" shows, first of all, that O'Hara's affirmation in "A Step Away from Them" was indeed tentative. While in "A Step Away from Them" the poet finds enough worth in his experience to offset his feeling of loss, in "Adieu to Norman" he doubts whether he will, in fact, be able to do so. It also discloses something of the value of Reverdy for O'Hara. What O'Hara values in Reverdy's work in "Adieu to Norman" is his affirmation that "everything continues to be possible" and that, in particular, it is possible to find sufficient value in one's own experience alone to warrant one's decision to continue to live.

While after the moment of crisis O'Hara becomes interested in his present experience, which displaces the feeling of loss he feels, he must return to work where, unlike in the street of his lunch hour, there are fewer distractions. While his lunch hour was a moment of escape, the risk is that his feeling of loss will return once he returns to his office, and life will seem banal and pointless. The value of Reverdy's work, however, is that it sustains his interest in, and his feeling of exhilaration with, his own experience, and is, therefore, a tacit statement that his experience will be full enough to continue with life in spite of the pain that it produces.

Art does this, in part, in providing a form for experience that is new and surprising. In "Digression on *Number 1*, 1948" (1956), for example, which was written six months after "A Step Away from Them," O'Hara shows how Pollock's work, as well as that of Joan Miró (1893–1983), Fernand Léger (1881–1955), Jean Metzinger (1883–1956), Victor Brauner (1903–66), and Picasso, reinvigorates his present experience by renewing his perception of color, light, and form:

DIGRESSION ON *NUMBER 1, 1948*

I am ill today but I am not
too ill. I am not ill at all.
It is a perfect day, warm
for winter, cold for fall.

A fine day for seeing. I see
ceramics, during lunch hour, by
Miró, and I see the sea by Léger;
light, complicated Metzingers
and a rude awakening by Brauner,
a little table by Picasso, pink.

I am tired today but I am not
too tired. I am not tired at all.
There is the Pollock, white, harm
will not fall, his perfect hand

and the many short voyages. They'll
never fence the silver range.
Stars are out and there is sea
enough beneath the glistening earth
to bear me toward the future
which is not so dark. I see.

(*CP*, 260)

While the poet begins the day feeling both "ill" and "tired," the art he sees in the course of his day renews his sense of dimension and texture ("ceramics"), objects ("the sea by Léger"), paradox ("light, complicated Metzingers"), intensity ("a rude awakening by Brauner"), and color and size ("a little table by Picasso, pink"). The works he observes remind him of the seemingly infinite complexities of his visual and emotional experience and give him the feeling that the world produces a sufficient variety and number of experiences ("there is sea / enough beneath the glistening earth") to occupy his attention and interest for the duration of his life. Hence, the future "is not so dark" after all.

O'Hara demonstrates in language the sense of renewal these works of art create. In the cubist paintings of Picasso and Léger, objects and forms are placed on the canvas in such a manner as to detach them from the normal contexts in which each object or form is seen and to create a new object, the painting itself. This produces a heightened sense of the colors, forms, and texture that constitute each object, and embodies the different perspectives from which we can observe our experience. O'Hara does the same thing with the words of "Digression on *Number 1*, 1948." In his choice of placement and word order, O'Hara draws attention to the words themselves as words, to the states of affairs and concepts each word represents and to the multiple meanings each word possesses. In doing so, he reinvigorates our sense of the meaning of words and makes apparent the complex nature of our experience.

The play of "see" and "sea," for example, in "I see the sea by Léger" attracts attention to both the phonemes and the letters that constitute the words themselves, as well as to the difference in meaning between the two words. His use of "light" in the line "light, complicated Metzingers" could refer both to an absence of darkness and to a casual air. In the case of the second meaning, O'Hara describes a paradox represented in Metzinger's work, which further draws attention to the words on the page. The separation of the adjective "pink" from the phrase "little table by Picasso" separates the color from the object and hence draws our attention to the word "pink" and the color pink. It is as if we perceive two entities—first at a little table and then a pink table—at separate moments in time, which, in the end, turn out to be the same object. And in his description of Pollock's painting, while the word "white" describes the color of the painting, its position before the noun "harm" allows us to read it as an adjective that describes "harm." This is further encouraged when we read the following line and observe that "harm" can also be read as a pun on "arm" in order to parallel the expression "perfect hand," which appears at the end of the subsequent line.

Art, in this sense, teaches us how to experience time. In "Getting up ahead of Someone (Sun)" (1959), the sole place that he ever used the phrase, "I do this I do that," O'Hara examines the relationship between art and time. In this poem, O'Hara writes of getting up before dawn and watching the day begin rather than "grabbing on late as usual" (*CP*, 341). What he feels is a sense of peace and a sense of fullness. He is "not tired not nervous," but rather "truly awake" as he experiences each moment of time in all its fullness. He writes:

> the light flows evenly along the lawn
> in chilly Southampton and I smoke
> and hours and hours go by I read
> van Vechten's *Spider Boy* then a short
> story by Patsy Southgate and a poem
> by myself
>
> (*CP*, 341)

As Hans-Georg Gadamer notes in "The Relevance of the Beautiful," both boredom and overbusyness are, in the end, experiences of time as an object in and of itself rather than the medium in which we experience other things.[10] Here, the fact that time passes almost without notice shows that it is not the object of experience and that each moment is neither too long (which would lead to boredom and a direct experience of time) nor too short (which would lead to overbusyness). It is this experience of time that he expresses in his "sketch pad":

> and the house wakes up and goes
> to get the dog in Sag Harbor I make
> myself a bourbon and commence
> to write one of my "I do this I do that"
> poems in a sketch pad
> it is tomorrow
> though only six hours have gone by
> each day's light has more significance these days
>
> (*CP*, 341)

While each day's light has "more significance" because of the fact that there are but six hours of it on this particular day, O'Hara implies that art provides his time with such significance. In the end, O'Hara draws a comparison between his experience of time when he gets up before dawn and the experience of time that is produced when he "tarries," to borrow Gadamer's term, over works of art.[11] The reference to his "I do this I do that" poems in this context is a tacit statement of the purpose of these poems to, in effect, express his experience in a form via naming that allows him to experience each moment in all its fullness rather than as a moment of loss.

This use of both common and proper names to capture or create the fullness of time is present in "The Day Lady Died" as well. Yet, it is also a poem in which O'Hara uses naming to establish a context for feeling that is authentic.

THE DAY LADY DIED

It is 12:20 in New York a Friday
three days after Bastille day, yes
it is 1959 and I go get a shoeshine
because I will get off the 4:19 in Easthampton
at 7:15 and then go straight to dinner
and I don't know the people who will feed me

I walk up the muggy street beginning to sun
and have a hamburger and a malted and buy
an ugly NEW WORLD WRITING to see what the poets
in Ghana are doing these days
                    I go on to the bank
and Miss Stillwagon (first name Linda I once heard)
doesn't even look up my balance for once in her life
and in the GOLDEN GRIFFIN I get a little Verlaine
for Patsy with drawings by Bonnard although I do
think of Hesiod, trans. Richmond Lattimore or
Brendan Behan's new play or *Le Balcon* or *Les Nègres*
of Genet, but I don't, I stick with Verlaine
after practically going to sleep with quandariness

and for Mike I just stroll into the PARK LANE
Liquor Store and ask for a bottle of Strega and
then I go back where I came from to 6th Avenue
and the tobacconist in the Ziegfeld Theatre and
casually ask for a carton of Gauloises and a carton
of Picayunes, and a NEW YORK POST with her face on it

and I am sweating a lot by now and thinking of
leaning on the john door in the 5 SPOT

while she whispered a song along the keyboard
to Mal Waldron and everyone and I stopped breathing

(*CP*, 325)

"The Day Lady Died" is first and foremost an elegy for the late jazz singer Billie Holiday. O'Hara heard Holiday sing on two occasions. The first time was in the summer of 1957, when she performed in the Loew's Sheridan on Seventh Avenue and Twelfth Street.[12] She was not allowed to perform in a bar that served alcoholic beverages because of an arrest for possession of heroin and, therefore, had to sing in the old movie theater at the Sheridan.[13] The second and last time he heard her sing was at the Five Spot, a jazz bar on Fifth Street and Third Avenue. Mal Waldron, Holiday's accompanist on piano, often played there, and Holiday showed up one night to visit him. Kenneth Koch and Frank O'Hara were there that evening, and Koch recalls: "It was very close to the end of her life, with her voice almost gone, just like a whisper, just like the taste of very old wine, but full of spirit. Everybody wanted her to sing. Everybody was crazy about her. She sang some songs in this very whispery beautiful voice. The place was quite crowded. Frank was standing near the toilet door so he had a side view. And Mal Waldron was at the piano. She sang these songs and it was very moving."[14] It is clearly this second performance to which O'Hara refers in the poem.

"The Day Lady Died" is an elegy of the most sensitive kind in that O'Hara does not presume to either sum up Holiday's life or impart some ultimate meaning to her death. Such efforts would, in the end, only be reductive and do both her life and death injustice. Rather he re-creates in the poem how she affected him: when she sang, she took his breath away. O'Hara avoids sentimentality by saying this indirectly. He does not mention Billie Holiday by name. Rather, he uses her nickname, "Lady Day," in the title, and refers to her for the first time in the poem itself by referring to "a NEW YORK POST with her face on it," and in the final section of the poem, where there is his most explicit reference to her, he refers to her as "she." His references, furthermore, to "the poets of Ghana" and Jean Genet's *Les Nègres* as works of art that represent Africans in a postcolonial world accept a second significance as metaphors for Holiday's whispering, which, because of the delay, make them much more subtle and authentic. The last line of the poem becomes truly mimetic, as Marjorie Perloff has pointed out, in that it imitates the feeling of shock and loss at discovering that someone you know has died (*FOH*, 181). It is worth noting that this feeling is further emphasized in the lack of a period, which prolongs the pause at the end of the poem.

In naming things, O'Hara prevents the poem from becoming too "reflective" or dense with what he calls "emotional spilling over" (*CP*, 497). This would make the poem into "the typical poem of a self-pitying or infatuated writer" (*SS*, 35). Rather, in naming the things and events of his lunch hour, he is able to use the small shift in tone and in language in the final lines to its fullest effect. This small shift expresses a feeling of loss and admiration in an authentic and effective way. In short, by avoiding direct references to Holiday and using works of art as metaphors to foreshadow the ultimate significance of Holiday's music, as well as naming in order to use a subtle shift in tone to great effect, O'Hara avoids the vulgarity of overextravagant expression of emotion, and creates an effective and authentic elegy.

Thus, O'Hara uses proper names to establish a formal and psychological context without which his poetic, final line would not have the authentic, emotive impact it does. In Goodman's terms, O'Hara uses both common proper names and ordinary events to ground the poem in "real and detailed subject-matter," and, therefore, to establish the final emotive line of the poem as "plausible."[15]

In the first four sections of the poem, for example, we observe an "I" that is surrounded by experience that is, perhaps, ordinary. His lunch hour is scheduled with a number of everyday tasks that he must do to prepare for his evening with friends. He gets a shoeshine, eats a quick lunch, goes to the bank, and buys gifts during his lunch hour because he will need to leave right after work to catch the 4:19 train to Easthampton. At the end of the fourth section, however, the poem has come full circle. The poet has returned to where he came from, "to 6th Avenue / and the tobacconist in the Ziegfeld Theatre." The first four sections, therefore, constitute a whole, which O'Hara separates from the final section, thus contrasting the dramatic moment in the final section with the ultimate normalcy of the rest of his day. This dramatic moment is triggered when the poet sees "a NEW YORK POST with her face on it," informing him of Billie Holiday's death. In a moment where time seems suspended, he recalls hearing her whisper "a song along the keyboard / to Mal Waldron," and the "breathlessness" he feels as he realizes that she has died (as well as the breathlessness he feels from walking around town) fuses with the breathlessness he felt when he heard her sing at the FiveSpot two years earlier.

"The Day Lady Died," however, is not only a poem about Billie

Holiday. It is also a poem in which O'Hara underlines the value of poetry in restoring—though only momentarily—the initial but faded experience of the things named in it. The problem with our experience of things is that, like the things themselves, it fades. In his journal in 1949, O'Hara writes: "The fragility of things terrifies me! However belligerent the cactus, ash from a casual cigarette withers its bloom; the blackest puddle greys at the first drop of rain; everything fades fades changes dies when it's meddled with; if only things weren't so vulnerable! We're all children playing naked in the sun!" (*EW*, 109).

Things do not remain the same, but are changed with the slightest interaction with other things. The cactus becomes less beautiful because of a "casual cigarette," and a black puddle becomes a sort of polluted gray because of a drop of rain. His experience changes with these things, and O'Hara's fear is that this change is one of degeneration. He no longer perceives, for example, the beauty of the cactus in blossom once it has "withered." His experience of the sharply defined black puddle is gone once the rain falls. Everything O'Hara writes, "fades fades changes dies," which, in turn, reminds him of his own fragility: "We're all children playing naked in the sun!" The value of poetry, and art in general, however, for O'Hara, is that it renews his sense of these faded experiences by re-creating them in the present, which may not stop the process of degeneration, but nevertheless slows it.

Thus, naming things in O'Hara's work is part of an effort to create poems that allow the poet to express authentic moments of feeling that revitalize one's experience of the world—past and present. In poems such as "A Step away from Them" and "The Day Lady Died," O'Hara shows us that the pleasure we obtain from the experience of things—both the everyday and the extraordinary—affirms our sense of being. The artist, O'Hara claims in 1949, attempts "to give his time what it needs": "caught in the flood of destruction which is our historical milieu, he wonders where to place his sandbag most efficaciously; if his judgment is wrong, at least he stood on the levee, at least he used his judgment, at least he had a sandbag" (*EW*, 97).

Naming things is one of O'Hara's most valuable sandbags. It is an affirmation of the value of our experience of things and events in response to the seeming meaninglessness and boredom of life, and a tacit statement of the value of art in postponing fear of loss and death.

The importance placed on poetry's experiential function in the present work, however, begs the question as to who or what feels. Thus, it is to O'Hara's understanding of the self that we will now turn.

4

The Self and "In Memory of My Feelings"

IT IS OFTEN ARGUED THAT "IN MEMORY OF MY FEELINGS" (1956) IS O'Hara's most accomplished autobiographical poem. For example, Marjorie Perloff writes that "In Memory of My Feelings" is "not only O'Hara's best autobiographical poem, but one of the great poems of our time" (*FOH*, 141). For Perloff, this is because it is a poem in which O'Hara traces "the fragmentation and reintegration of the inner self" in a language that "turns the autobiographical convention inside out, fusing fantasy and realism in a painterly collage-poem, whose form is at one with its meaning" (141). "Few poets," Perloff argues, "could manage the difficult structural and textual modulations of this poem" (146). Similarly, Mutlu Konuk Blasing writes that "In Memory of My Feelings" "marks a significant point" in O'Hara's career where, she claims, he transcends "the Romantic dichotomy of Art and Life."[1] He does so, she argues, in creating a poem that treats the events of the poet's life as mere fodder for artistic expression, but also preserves these events and provides them with coherence. And Eric Mottram describes "In Memory of My Feelings" as a "1956 song of myself," in which O'Hara affirms the self over "art, transience, the hunter and the condition of being hunted."[2] For these critics, in "In Memory of My Feelings" O'Hara affirms this singular and continuous self over the "fragmentation" (Perloff), the "isolated moments of consciousness" (Blasing), and the "transience" (Mottram) that characterize the multiple self.

While these critics are correct that the central tension in the poem is between the self as multiple and changing and the self as "continuous and coherent," and that O'Hara transcends "Art and Life" in the poem, it is not a poem in which O'Hara "salvages" some continuous self. This is a reading that is largely dependent on understanding O'Hara's "serpent" in the final lines of the poem as a reference to a singular and continuous self. The "serpent" in O'Hara's poems, however, most often represents the artist or poet, not the "essential" or "continuous" self. In "In Memory of My Feelings," the self is both multiple and singular; but it is impossible to represent or express the self as continuous because it is not a constant object of perception (such as a noumenal self or a soul) but rather a creative force. For O'Hara, what is singular in the self, in other words, is its creative force that assimilates each added isolated moment of consciousness into a temporal, aggregate whole. Thus, at the end of "In Memory of My Feelings," O'Hara does not determine to salvage some coherent or continuous self from his past experiences (from what he calls "history" in the poem); rather, he determines to express the temporal manifestations of the self in his poems. This will, he hopes, "realize" the creative force within himself, and, therefore, "save the serpent" (namely, the poet, or the creative force that is at work within him). Before we turn to the poem, however, a brief examination of the self in O'Hara's other poems is needed.

The Self

While the self is indeed real for O'Hara, and, therefore, presented as a singular thing, what is most singular in the self is the creative force at the "center" of it that re-creates the self anew with each new experience. In other words, what is most singular and most unchanging in the self is the creative action of its constant becoming. In his short "Autobiographia Literaria" (1949), for example, O'Hara both parodies and follows Coleridge's definition of the imagination in *Biographia Literaria* (1813) as "the living Power and prime Agent of all human Perception, and as a repetition in the infinite I AM."[3] The poem begins with the poet reflecting on his childhood, and, in particular, his relationship to nature:

> When I was a child
> I played by myself in a
> corner of the schoolyard
> all alone.
>
> I hated dolls and I
> hated games, animals were
> not friendly and birds
> flew away.

> If anyone was looking
> for me I hid behind a
> tree and cried out "I am
> an orphan."
>
> (*CP*, 11)

Unlike Wordsworth and Coleridge, who present childhood as a moment of communion with the natural world, O'Hara's childhood is marked by alienation. He plays by himself "in a corner" and "all alone." In fact, his whole childhood is presented here as a period of isolation from others. Like Rilke, the child even hates dolls, presumably because they remind him of death.[4]

In the final stanza of the poem, however, the "I" of the poem comes to the fore. O'Hara writes:

> And here I am, the
> center of all beauty!
> Writing these poems!
> Imagine!
>
> (*CP*, 11)

While there is a fair amount of parodying of the thirteenth and fourteenth chapters of Coleridge's *Biographia Literaria* in these lines, in particular in O'Hara's juxtaposition of the phrase "I am" with the words "beauty" and "Imagine," he nevertheless expresses what is, in the end, true for him: writing is not an act of regaining a childlike communion with and perception of the world, but rather an act of creating, or coming into contact with, one's self. Poetry is, as O'Hara would later write in "To Gottfried Benn," "an instinct for self-declaration" (*CP*, 310).

In fact, O'Hara views the self and artistic creation to be so close as to be almost indistinguishable from one another. This is clear in both "A Note to Harold Foundren" (1950) and "Grand Central" (1953). O'Hara writes in "A Note to Harold Foundren," for example, that "We seed / the land and its art without being prodigal / and are ourselves its necessity and flower," and in "Grand Central" that "I am / reconstructed from a model of poetry" (*CP*, 34, 168). O'Hara's remarks here are evocative of Nietzsche's famous remarks in *The Birth of Tragedy* regarding the effects of the "Dionysian" in early Greek tragedy. Nietzsche writes: "Man is no longer an artist, he has become a work of art: the artistic power of all nature here reveals itself in the tremors of drunkenness to the highest gratification of the Primordial

Unity."[5] For Nietzsche, as numerous critics have noted, the Apollonian and the Dionysian forces in early Greek tragedy represent, respectively, the rational, self-definition of the individual and the participation in the chaotic, selfless oneness of all things. Christoph Cox writes, for example, that the "Apollonian affirms the *principium individuationis*, 'the delimiting boundaries of the individual, measure in the Hellenic sense.' The Dionysian, by contrast, affirms 'the mysterious primordial unity,' 'the shattering of the individual and his fusion with primordial being.' "[6] As Adrian Del Caro has noted, Nietzsche does not wish the Dionysian to replace the Apollonian in the arts, but rather he wants the balance between the two to be restored. His passion for the Dionysian can give the impression that it is the superior element in the arts, a position later adopted in the theories of the surrealists.[7] In the same passage Nietzsche states that in singing Beethoven's "jubilee-song" we come into contact with the Dionysian creative force, expressing what he calls "Primordial Unity." For his part, O'Hara claims that in "singing" he becomes an instrument of nature, or this primordial force at work in nature.

For O'Hara, however, this creative center or ground is not some Hegelian Absolute Spirit, but is characterized as the "emptiness of living." For example, in "Life on Earth" (1953), a poem in which O'Hara, not unsurprisingly, examines the cycle of life and death as part of the great creative act of the universe of which, according to O'Hara, we are all subjects, he writes that he is like a tree, clinging "to the emptiness of living which is his ground" (*CP*, 158). And in "Anacrostic" (1954), O'Hara writes that he is never "more than my immeasurable self / enchanting the yellow trees with my emptiness" (*CP*, 175). This metaphor of the creative ground being "the emptiness of living" is the basis of O'Hara's numerous references to the artist as a "pierced" and hollow tree that creates music as the wind passes through him, where the wind is a moment of feeling, and the music the "voice" or temporal self-expression of the poet.

The notion of the "ground" of the self as, ironically, "the emptiness of living"—which is to say, the accumulated, temporal, conscious events that are themselves the constituent parts of the self—is expressed elsewhere in O'Hara's poems when he remarks that the events that one experiences as being "outside" the self are, in fact, the constituent parts of the self. In "Ode to Michael Goldberg ('s Birth and Other Births)" (1958), for example, O'Hara notes, "in a forest you think of birds, in traffic you think of tires" (*CP*, 290). Examining this notion in more detail in "On Rachmaninoff's Birthday #158" (1961), O'Hara writes:

> but you get stuck in a habit
> of thinking about things
>   and realize they are all you
> that's amusing, hein?
> so think
>
> (*CP*, 418)

And in "Essay on Style" (1961), where O'Hara refigures thinking as the reflection of the material world on the poet, he writes: "I was reflecting the other night meaning / I was being reflected upon" (*CP*, 393). In each instance, O'Hara questions the facile distinction between me and not-me, inner and outer.

Because the self is grounded in the conscious events of life itself, it is, for O'Hara, something that is both multiple and changing. In "Poem (All the mirrors in the world)" (1950), O'Hara explores the notion that each new experience changes the self and, therefore, makes it impossible for the poet or artist to capture the whole self in his work because of the self's relationship to time. He writes:

> All the mirrors in the world
> don't help, nor am I moved
>
> by the calm emergence of my
> image in the rain, it is not
> I who appears or imagines.
>
> (*CP*, 39)

As the poem continues, his image, in fact, reminds him of past experiences, past selves, that seem to force themselves upon him and, therefore, serve to represent who he was and not who he is or will become. Furthermore, in "To Jane; and in Imitation of Coleridge" (1954), O'Hara muses on the seeming chaotic nature of himself as multiple (*CP*, 183). He writes:

> And I am all at sea, at war,
> if I ever had a chance I left it
> there on the iron deck, my star:
>   I strike upon, but cannot heft it.

> But I should be master of my ship
> not just a member of the crew!
> though she may think that I will slip
>   into insanity and blue
>
> (*CP*, 183)

The self is presented here as both an unstable, floating thing, "at sea, at war," and multiple in that it contains a whole crew of Frank O'Haras.

In this poem, however, the notion of the self as multiple and changing seems to make it impossible to live a "sane" life—which is to say, a life with some sort of continuous and coherent interaction between the self and the world. Recognizing this, O'Hara reassures Jane that he will not, in fact, "slip / into insanity." He is, he writes, "master" of himself. Ironically, however, he is not master of himself in the sense that he controls his multiple selves, unifying them in an act of the imagination to form a coherent whole. Rather, he is master of himself in the sense that he is free (i.e., as opposed to enslaved) to leave the ship behind if he so chooses and live a constantly *varied* life. He writes:

> I will not, for I more and more
> am master of myself each day,
> and sometimes from a savage shore
>   plunge into surf and swim away,
>
> (*CP*, 183)

To be "master" of oneself, therefore, for O'Hara, is to be free to follow the changing nature of one's feelings. This is, for O'Hara, a more honest recognition of who we are. As he writes in "My Heart" (1955):

> I'm not going to cry all the time
> nor shall I laugh all the time,
> I don't prefer one "strain" to another.
> I'd have the immediacy of a bad movie,
> not just a sleeper, but also the big,
> overproduced first-run kind. I want to be
> at least as alive as the vulgar. And if
> some aficionado of my mess says "That's
> not like Frank!", all to the good! I
> don't wear brown and grey suits all the time,
> do I? No. I wear workshirts to the opera,
> often. I want my feet to be bare,
> I want my face to be shaven, and my heart—

you can't plan on the heart, but
the better part of it, my poetry, is open.

(*CP*, 231)

To "be" oneself, in other words, is not to be constant and predictable; it is to be willing to accept each new feeling, no matter how much it makes "sense," as part of one's self. It is to be willing, as he writes in "In Memory of My Feelings," to "live as variously as possible" (*CP*, 256).

This understanding of the self as both the result of the creative force of nature and the temporal aggregate of all of one's previous selves is an understanding of the self that O'Hara shares with Alfred North Whitehead. O'Hara was familiar with Whitehead's cosmology as early as 1951 when he wrote "A Pleasant Thought from Whitehead," which is a play on Whitehead's *Modes of Thought* (1938). Whitehead, furthermore, was an important influence on a number of artists that influenced O'Hara—including both Gertrude Stein and Robert Motherwell (the latter studied under Whitehead at Harvard). In *Process and Reality* (1929), Whitehead provides an explanation of what he calls "actual entities," which are the constituent parts of the world. Whitehead writes: "'Actual entities'—also termed 'actual occasions'—are the final real things of which the world is made up. There is no going behind actual entities to find anything more real. . . . The final acts are, all alike, actual entities; and these actual entities are drops of experience, complex and interdependent."[8]

The first thing to note with respect to Whitehead's definition of "actual entities" as "drops of experience" is that it is a definition, as Victor Lowe remarks, that rejects the Newtonian understanding of existence in terms of material substance.[9] For Whitehead, existence is analogous to experience, which, in turn, refers to all material and cognitive events. Thus, Lowe notes, mass no longer refers to a "permanent quantity of matter," but is rather, in Whitehead's conception of it, "'the name for a quantity of energy considered in relation to some of its dynamical effects'; and energy 'is merely the name for the quantitative aspect of a structure of happenings.'"[10] Thus Whitehead states: "[H]ow an actual entity *becomes* constitutes *what* that actual entity *is;* so that the two descriptions of an actual entity are not independent. Its 'being' is constituted by its 'becoming.' This is the 'principle of process.'"[11] To "be" a self or an actual entity, then, is to "be" something that is always changing and becoming with each new "drop of experience." There are, Whitehead writes, "no novel eternal objects."[12]

Each new "drop of experience" does not eradicate the previous events actualized in a moment of time, but is dependent on them for its own actualization, as well as the nexus of actualized entities that make up the world as a whole at a given moment. Each new experience creates the self anew not from a tabula rasa, but through bringing together the current self with some other thing outside the self in the mind of an individual. This bringing together is the creative "event," or new actualization of the self.

While there is no continuous self for Whitehead, there is a continual and universal process, which is the process of creation, of self-actualization. This process is one of Whitehead's universal categories, along with "many" and "one," which he understands as replacing Aristotle's, as well as much of Western philosophy's, ontology. Whitehead writes:

> The ultimate metaphysical principle is the advance from disjunction to conjunction, creating a novel entity other than the entities given in disjunction. The novel entity is at once the togetherness of the "many" which it finds, and also it is one among the disjunctive "many" which it leaves; it is a novel entity, disjunctively among the many entities which it synthesizes. The many become one, and are increased by one. In their natures, entities are disjunctively "many" in process of passage into conjunctive unity. This Category of the Ultimate replaces Aristotle's category of "primary substance."[13]

Thus, what we have with Whitehead is an ontology of creative movement from disjunction to conjunction, and a constantly changing nexus of relations between individual entities and the aggregate whole.

There is a corresponding tension in O'Hara's understanding of the self (and in Whitehead's thought). On the one hand, the self is a real, individual thing, an expression of a constant and continuous creative force. On the other hand, because of the fact that the self is the result of a creative force, it is something that is always changing, and that can be understood as the temporal aggregate of an accumulated number of feelings and experiences. It is thus both continuous and discontinuous, both part of a larger whole (which is the creative force of nature itself) and a distinct, albeit temporal, thing, separate from, or at least distinguishable from, other selves and other instances of "creation" in nature.

While a number of poets have espoused an analogous view of the self, what is different with O'Hara is his commitment to the temporal manifestations of the self in his work. The problem with the surrealists for O'Hara, as well as for other American artists, is that, at least in Breton's vision of surrealism, the ground of the self located in the unconscious mind becomes the principal object of the expressive act to the exclusion of the particular, temporal manifestations of this ground in the artist's actual life. For O'Hara, in contrast, the individual self matters, however temporal or fractured. The experiences of the temporal self, for O'Hara, are the object of art.

"In Memory of My Feelings"

In "In Memory of My Feelings," O'Hara presents the self as both singular and multiple in the beginning of the poem, and does not move to a more univocal presentation of the self at the end of the poem. Rather, O'Hara reflects on the relationship of his various past selves to his current self. He examines how these past selves, or past feelings, are both dead and alive in the sense that they continue to be part of who he is in the present. He examines two models of how to relate the past and the present—that of the "Arabs" and that of the "Greeks"—and determines, in the end, that both are impossible. Therefore, rather than constructing some "coherent" self out of his multiple selves, he determines to transform them into art and, therefore, "save" himself as a work of art.

In the first section of the poem, O'Hara presents the "I" of the poem as both singular and multiple, and addresses the problem of writing an autobiographical poem that is open, but not too open, in order to protect himself from being attacked by "creatures" who "have murder in their heart" (*CP*, 253). O'Hara begins:

> My quietness has a man in it, he is transparent
> and he carries me quietly, like a gondola, through the streets.
> He has several likenesses, like stars and years, like numerals.
> My quietness has a number of naked selves
>
> (*CP*, 252)

The poet's "quietness" can be understood to refer to the external self, and the "man" that it contains to refer to the internal self. In this opening section, he characterizes the man in his "quietness" as "transparent," multiple, and naked. Yet, this internal, multiple man, who is both naked and transparent, "carries" the poet's external "quietness" "like a gondola, through the streets." Furthermore, the poet's "quietness" is also said to be multiple; it possesses "several likenesses," which, O'Hara points out, are not mere copies but "like stars and years, like numerals." While Perloff (*FOH*, 142) argues that O'Hara, in these lines, reveals that "Frank O'Hara the 'poet' is still dominated by Frank O'Hara the man who carries him 'quietly, like a gondola, through the streets,'" it seems rather that O'Hara is concerned with showing that he is, in fact, multiple, and that there is no seamless distinction between singular and multiple or between inner and outer selves.

No sooner has O'Hara referred to his selves as "naked" than he introduces the need to protect his selves from a number of unidentified "creatures":

> so many pistols I have borrowed to protect myselves
> from creatures who too readily recognize my weapons
> and have murder in their heart!
>
> (*CP*, 253)

These "creatures" are hunters, whom O'Hara identifies as his dead family in section 2 and "our democracy" in section 5 (*CP*, 253, 256). While O'Hara does not tell us how these hunters hope to "murder" his selves, it may be that "murder" is a metaphor for the refusal of his family to recognize his selves as genuine. Hence, the poet must protect himself with "pistols," a metaphor that O'Hara used on occasion to refer to either his own poems or the work of other artists—as he does, for example, in "Poem (I ran through the snow like a young Czarevitch)" (1951). His poems protect his selves in a couple of ways. On the one hand, as concrete artifacts of intangible phenomena (i.e., the poet's feelings), his poems affirm his selves as real. On the other hand, his poems hide his self from potential murders. Furthermore, as O'Hara notes later in the poem, they attack the hunters themselves by reshaping the values of the world in such a manner that his selves can to be accepted.

This twofold action of self-declaration and defense in "In Memory of My Feelings" is enacted in the lines directly following his recognition of these dangerous "creatures." O'Hara describes his selves as roses, a mountain, a spectator at a racetrack, a jockey, and a bird, perhaps a pink flamingo, in the middle of the track:

> One of me rushes
> to window # 13 and one of me raises his whip and one of me
> flutters up from the center of the track amidst the pink flamingoes,

> and underneath their hooves as they round the last turn my lips
> are scarred and brown, brushed by tails, masked in dirt's lust,
> definition, open mouths gasping for the cries of the bettors for the lungs
> of the earth.
>
> (*CP*, 253)

Perloff is correct, I believe, when she writes that the poet seems to remember "moments of unspecified but terrible humiliation" (*FOH*, 143). However, while there is a vague sense of terror that is expressed in these lines, we do not have the details of the event, but rather the poet's associated images.

The image of the serpent at the end of the first section underscores the dialectic of self-declaration and defense. O'Hara writes:

> I am underneath its leaves as the hunter crackles and pants
> and bursts, as the barrage balloon drifts behind a cloud
> and animal death whips out its flashlight,
>   whistling
> and slipping the glove off the trigger hand. The serpent's eyes
> redden at the sight of those thorny fingernails, he is so smooth!
>
> (*CP*, 253)

The serpent, enacting the protection that comes from being obscure or unrecognized, hides as the hunter walks around the forest shooting and searching for prey. While he remains hidden, however, he does not move, and as the hunter removes his gloves, the serpent's eyes "redden" as if to prepare to attack, thus asserting his prerogative to remain present.

As mentioned, Perloff has argued that the serpent stands for O'Hara's true self, but it is clear from O'Hara's references to it throughout the rest of the poem, as well as his references to "serpents," "vipers," and "snakes" in other poems, that it stands for the poet, who in "In Memory of My Feelings" is the prey of his family and of society, what O'Hara will call later "our democracy," but also a predator able to strike back at both. After the above image of the serpent and the hunter, O'Hara ends the first section of the poem with a description of these "transparent selves" that flail about "like vipers in a pail":

>   My transparent selves
> flail about like vipers in a pail, writhing and hissing

without panic, with a certain justice of response
and presently the aquiline serpent comes to resemble the Medusa.
(*CP*, 253)

While the description of his "selves" as "vipers" might suggest that, as Perloff argues, "the serpent" should be understood as his "true self," in the midst of these "vipers," O'Hara writes that "the aquiline serpent comes to resemble the Medusa." The reference to Medusa is important, for she is the mother of Pegasus, who is often associated with the arts. Thus, we have a picture of the poet as a serpent that resembles Medusa in the midst of his "selves" that flail about "like vipers," rather than some "true self" in the midst of fragmented versions of himself.

These final lines of the first section are evocative of Rilke's description of himself as a young poet in the "Third Elegy" of the *Duino Elegies*, where he recounts the painful transition from an "entangled" "interior world" to a violent exterior world that was "still gorged with father." Rilke writes:

So young and shy, how he entangled himself
in the spreading roots of events inside him,
twisted patterns, strangling, tendrils, shapes
of preying animals. How he surrendered.—Loved.
Loved his interior world, the jungle in him, that
primal inner forest where his pale green heart stood
among the fallen and mute ruins. Loved. Then left it,
going out from his own roots into violent Beginning
where his own tiny birth was already outlived. Loving,
he stepped down into the older blood, into the canyons
where terror lurked, still gorged with fathers.
And every horror knew him, winked, and seemed to
understand[14]

The entanglement of O'Hara's "transparent selves" around the poet is very much akin to Rilke's poet here in the "Third Elegy" who loves his "entangled" interior world, which he, in turn, surrenders to step out into "violent Beginning." The hunter in O'Hara's final lines who whistles and smoothly slips his glove off "the trigger hand," revealing his "thorny fingernails" in the process of preparing to shoot, is evocative of the "terror" in Rilke, lurking in the outer world, where "every horror knew" the young poet already, "winked, and seemed to / understand." In both cases, we have a young, "entangled" poet, facing an old, wise, violent foe—a foe, furthermore, that is, perhaps, part family.

O'Hara does not return to the serpent until the final sections of the poem, where he uses it, as he did in the first section, as a metaphor for the poet. For example, he begins the fifth section with the lines:

> And now it is the serpent's turn.
> I am not quite you, but almost, the opposite of visionary.
> You are coiled around the central figure,
>   the heart
>
> (*CP*, 256)

Not only is there a clear distinction between the "I" of the poem in these lines, which is not the poet, and the serpent, but the serpent possesses the stereotypical poetic quality of feeling. He is, for example, "coiled around the central figure / the heart" and, O'Hara writes, is moved by feeling, bubbling "with red ghosts, since to move is to love / and the scrutiny of all things is syllogistic" (*CP*, 256).

The coil of the serpent is itself circular, figuring the ironic use of a sort of syllogism in the following lines, from which the serpent scrutinizes the heart. In fact, feeling seems to be the serpent's defining quality:

>   When you turn your head
> can you feel your heels, undulating? that's what it is
> to be a serpent. I haven't told you of the most beautiful things
> in my lives, and watching the ripple of their loss disappear
> along the shore, underneath ferns
>
> (*CP*, 256)

To feel movement (and, therefore love) is what it means "to be a serpent." It is the serpent, furthermore, that not only feels, but also expresses and withholds, his memories ("I haven't told you of the most beautiful things").

O'Hara's depiction, furthermore, of the serpent as both a prey and a predator makes more sense in the context of the poem if we understand it to be referring to O'Hara the poet rather than to O'Hara's "true self." While the serpent is indeed a "prey" in that it can be "killed" by the hunter, it can, in turn, strike back in becoming like "a great Courbet," bending "the ear of the outer world":

but the prey
is always fragile and like something, as a seashell can be
a great Courbet, if it wishes. To bend the ear of the outer world.
(*CP*, 256)

This comparison to the work of Gustave Courbet (1819–77), who painted actual human figures and real events rather than using models to depict historical or mythological events or characters, and whose work was first condemned as ugly and lacking in imagination—as was the case with his *L'atelier du peintre* (1854–55), for example—but later hailed as revolutionary, states in no uncertain terms O'Hara's hope that his poems, like the painting of Courbet and like the poems of Cavalcanti, define rather than conform to current notions of aesthetic value in art and current notions of what is moral and what is not.[15] The serpent, therefore, is a predator in that it changes the outer world so that he is no longer hunted. In this sense, his art is an attack or a form of defense against the "hunter."

It is also worth noting that when O'Hara refers to "the serpent" or "snakes" in other poems, he never uses it as a metaphor for his "true self." In "Oranges: Twelve Pastorals," O'Hara writes that "Pan made vivid the pink and white hunger of my senses," after which he becomes a figure in the midst of "snakes twined about my limbs" (*CP*, 7). In the poem "The Lover" (c. 1950), O'Hara refers to the poet (presented as the lover of the material world) as standing in the midst of grass "full of snakespit," and he is alone, "hot amidst the stars" (*CP*, 46). In "Beach Party" (1952), he writes of "rattlers" that "serenaded each other," and in "Snapshot for Boris Pasternak" (1952) he refers to his childhood "sufferings" as being set among snakes: "The sufferings of my childhood were set / among these beauties, subtle as a snake" (*CP*, 96, 111). And in "Blue Territory" (1957), O'Hara writes of "THE SERPENT" whose "wailing is singing" and whose "curling anamores of the thigh" are "art nouveau kissings" (*CP*, 270–71). In each of these cases the poet's self is distinct from both serpents and snakes.

While, in the first section of the poem, O'Hara establishes the fact that he is both one and many, and introduces the serpent, which, like the poet, is both a prey and a predator in the violent outer world, O'Hara turns his attention in the second, third, and fourth sections to the relationship between his multiples selves. In the second section of the poem, for example, he remembers past selves, speaks of their "philosophical" death during his time in the U.S. Navy, and questions whether there is a true self that underlies all these versions of himself, while in sections 3 and 4, he reflects on two models of how to interact with his various past selves. He says he could follow the example of the Arabs and forget them, or he could follow the example of the Greeks and convert them into what he calls "history." Both of these models, however, are rejected, and O'Hara returns to the serpent in the fifth and final section, resolving to change these selves into art.

O'Hara begins the second section of the poem with reference to the fact that he is "ahunted" by his dead family:

> The dead hunting
> and the alive, ahunted.
> My father, my uncle,
> my grand-uncle and the several aunts. My
> grand-aunt dying for me, like a talisman, in the war,
> before I had even gone to Borneo
>
> (*CP*, 253)

While the poet sees his family as those who hunt him, he is aware of the fact that they see themselves as his protectors. His grand-aunt dies for him, for example, hoping that her death will bring him protection. Her death, however, is not effective. She dies for him before he has even gone to sea, and when he does go to sea, he is "hit":

> a rusted barge
> painted orange against the sea
> full of Marines reciting the Arabian ideas
> which are a proof in themselves of seasickness
> which is proof in itself of being hunted.
> A hit? *ergo* swim
> My 10 my 19,
> my 9, and the several years. My
> 12 years since they all died, philosophically speaking.
>
> (*CP*, 254)

This "hit" is not that of a real torpedo, but rather a philosophical one, which causes, in turn, the philosophical deaths of his "10," "19," and "9" selves—iconic versions of the multiple selves noted at the opening of the poem. That this philosophical "hit" took place during his time in the Navy is clear from the context of the passage as well as from the references to "a rusted barge," "Marines," "seasickness," and the need to "swim." Furthermore, O'Hara writes that it has been "12 years" since these selves died, which would mean that it took place when he was eighteen years old and in the Navy.[16]

In a paper for Albert Guérard at Harvard, O'Hara detailed his wartime experiences and wrote of a moment in the Navy when he realized that a particular life suited him more than the "given terms" according to which he had lived his life up until that moment. This is perhaps the "hit" that O'Hara refers to in the above passage:

> I found that I myself was my life . . . the person who cannot face himself enough to face the world on certain given terms may find that other terms are more suitable to his psyche: this is a matter of self-knowledge, not cowardice: there is no ivory tower; there are arrangements of the complex resulting from physical, intellectual, emotional, aesthetic sensitivities which dictate a particular way of life; but no one way of life is more valid than another; I had subconsciously felt this, and now I knew it. From that monstrous womb: a second birth. (*EW*, 122–23)

O'Hara felt that certain forces dictated the terms on which he would live his life, and that these terms were different from the ones he had been "given." His realization that "no one way of life is more valid than another," referring perhaps to his understanding of himself as a homosexual and his decision to live his life according to how he felt, was a "second birth."

While this realization is a moment of "celebration," it is also a moment of anxiety:

> And now the coolness of a mind
> like a shuttered suite in the Grand Hotel
> where mail arrives for my incognito,
>   whose façade
> has been slipping into the Grand Canal for centuries;
> rockets splay over a *sposalizio*,
>   fleeing into night
> from their Chinese memories, and it is a celebration,
> the trying desperately to count them as they die.
> But who will stay to be these numbers
> when all the lights are dead?
>
> (*CP*, 254)

At first, the death of these past selves produces a moment of peace. His mind is cool and at rest "like a shuttered suite in the Grand Hotel." This moment of peace, however, is precarious. Mail arrives for his "incognito," either reminding him his second birth as a homosexual is still secret or expressing doubt about the identity of the self that was created out of this second birth. The hotel's facade continues its slow slip "into the Grand Canal," creating the fear that should it slip it might reveal that this "shuttered suite in the Grand Hotel" is either occupied by a closet homosexual or empty, and that he is nobody. This double fear increases as he watches "rockets splay over a *sposalizio*" as he "desperately" tries "to count them as they die."

As mentioned, in the third and fourth sections of the poem O'Hara examines two possible models of how to relate to his past as well as present selves. The first is the example of the Arabs:

> You preferred the Arabs? but they didn't stay to count
> their inventions, racing into sands, converting themselves into
> so many,
>   embracing, at Ramadan, the tenderest effigies of
> themselves with penises shorn by the hundreds, like a camel
> ravishing a goat.
>
> (*CP*, 254)

The Arabs left the past unremembered to create a new (religious) version of themselves. The second model is the example of the Greeks, who separated the past from themselves and "converted" it into a concrete form:

>   And the mountainous-minded Greeks could speak
> of time as a river and step across it into Persia, leaving the pain
> at home to be converted into statuary.
>
> (*CP*, 254)

While the Greeks would acknowledge the continuous nature of time, they were nevertheless able to separate themselves from the past like the Arabs. The benefit of converting the past into a fixed form, however, is that as such it could not only be left "at home" and, therefore, separated from the new self, but also still provide a sense of connectedness with the past as a monument of it.

At first, O'Hara seems to approve of both models. He writes, for example, in the manner of Whitman's all-inclusive "I":

>   I adore the Roman copies.
> And the stench of the camel's spit I swallow,
> and the stench of the whole goat. For we have advanced, France,
> together into a new land, like the Greeks, where one feels nostalgic
> for mere ideas, where truth lies on its deathbed like an uncle
>
> (*CP*, 254)

However, as he examines the approach of the Greeks in the example of Lord Nelson, he raises the question of the relationship between the Lord Nelson that has been monumentalized and the real one (*CP*, 254). "How many selves," O'Hara asks, "are there in a war hero asleep in names?" (*CP*, 255). This is the question that he, in turn, asks of himself in the fourth section. For while he would like to follow the example of the Greeks and change his past "into history," defining it—and, therefore, providing himself with a means of separating himself from his past while still remaining connected to it—this is, in the end, too restrictive, for he is unable to give his past one form alone.

In the fourth section, O'Hara begins with a memory of visiting Jane Freilicher in Chicago five years earlier. He wakes up before her one morning and sees "a Norwegian freighter" with "a few dirty men, / tired of night," watching "themselves in the water" (*CP*, 255). As the men are looking at themselves in the water, he begins to shave, and, seeing his reflection in the mirror, his identity merges with them in the form of two Grace Hartigan paintings of him: *Ocean Bathers* (1953) and *Frank O'Hara and the Demons* (1952):

> One of me is standing in the waves, an ocean bather,
> or I am naked with a plate of devils at my hip.
>
> (*CP*, 255)[17]

After this moment of fusion, O'Hara assumes a number of different identities:

> Grace
> to be born and live as variously as possible. The conception
> of the masque barely suggests the sordid identifications.
> I am a Hittite in love with a horse. I don't know what blood's
> in me I feel like an African prince I am a girl walking downstairs
> in a red pleated dress with heels I am a champion taking a fall
> I am a jockey with a sprained ass-hole I am the light mist
> in which a face appears
> and it is another face of blonde I am a baboon eating a banana
> I am a dictator looking at his wife I am a doctor eating a child
> and child's mother smiling I am a Chinaman climbing a mountain
> I am a child smelling his father's underwear I am an Indian
> sleeping on a scalp
> and my pony is stamping in the birches,
> I've just caught sight of the *Niña*, the *Pinta* and the *Santa Maria*.
> What land is this so free?
>
> (*CP*, 256)

The multiple selves of the first section reappear in this penultimate section. As is the case in the first section, each of these selves is an expression of who he is. O'Hara writes that the "conception / of the masque barely suggests the sordid identifications." These are not roles that the "I" of the poem assumes, while some other continuous self exists in contradistinction to them, but rather expressions of his self and its multiple nature. These selves are expressions of the poet's "blood." All of them are expressions of some aspect of his concept of himself, but none of them is sufficient alone to represent the aggregate whole of who he is—which, for O'Hara, is, perhaps, always inexpressible.

Unlike the selves of the first section, however, these selves are not "scarred and brown," but bold, violent, and sexual. Each, furthermore, seems to exist in the present rather than in the past. Most of them are social outcasts of some sort. He is a "champion" that throws a fight, a jockey that cannot ride a horse, a dictator, "a doctor eating a child," and an "Indian / sleeping on a scalp" as the "whitemen" arrive on the *Niña*, *Pinta*, and *Santa Maria.* The clear sexual connotations of the images suggest that each one is an expression of O'Hara's sense of being a "sordid" other in a "democracy" that does not recognize him because of his homosexuality. He is, for example, a "girl walking downstairs," "a jockey with a sprained ass-hole," and "a baboon eating a banana." His rhetorical question "What land is this so free?" is stated when he is in the guise of an Indian watching Columbus arrive, and it discloses, that his relationship to this "democracy" is an antagonistic one. While the poet's selves, therefore, were hunted by his family in the first and second sections, in the fourth section his selves are hunted by the values (or presuppositions) of the society in which he lives.

Perloff claims that after this penultimate section, O'Hara leaves this multiple self (which she also sees as "fragmented") and, in the final section of the poem, affirms some sort of "coherent" or continuous self. She argues that O'Hara takes on these guises in the third and fourth section of the poem in an attempt to transcend the "fractured" nature of his "selves" (*FOH*, 144–45). The multiple and rapid associations lead to "a moment of ecstasy" where, she writes, the "fragmented self" is "reborn" and triumphs over the multiples selves in the poem (145–46). She sees this "moment" as occurring in the final lines of the poem, where O'Hara writes:

> and I have lost what is always and everywhere
> present, the scene of my selves, the occasion of these ruses,

which I myself and singly must now kill
and save the serpent in their midst.

(*CP*, 257)

Perloff writes that "in the 'midst' of all 'these ruses' is the serpent, who stands here for the poet's true self," which "must triumph if he is to become an artist" (*FOH*, 142, 146).

This reading, however, is based entirely on understanding O'Hara's use of the word "serpent" in the final line as a metaphor for his "true self," which, for Perloff, means an unfragmented self, which, a shown, does not square with O'Hara's use of the word elsewhere. It seems that rather than this being a poem in which O'Hara salvages some "coherent self" through art, it is one in which O'Hara determines to transform his feelings into art and, therefore, save himself as a poet.

O'Hara begins the final section of the poem by stating "And now it is the serpent's turn" (*CP*, 256). The poem has come full circle. This is the final identification. While the serpent, unlike the heroes of the third section, is "fragile" and a "prey" to hunters, it is also itself a predator:

the startled eyes of the dikdik, the bush full of white flags,
fleeing a hunter,
which is our democracy
but the prey
is always fragile and like something, as a seashell can be
a great Courbet, if it wishes. To bend the ear of the outer world.

(*CP*, 256)

While "our democracy" hunts the serpent, the serpent as poet is able to shape, or change, this "democracy" into something, it is implied, less dangerous. His poems, like "a great Courbet," shape the way others perceive the world, bending, as a seashell does, "the ear of the outer world." This change that the serpent accomplishes is, perhaps, a change in the values or presuppositions of those who constitute this "democracy."

Unlike the hero, furthermore, the poet continues to affect others, both in the present and in the future, after his death:

my body, the naked host to my many selves, shot
by a guerrilla warrior or dumped from a car into ferns
which are themselves *journalières.*
The hero, trying to unhitch his parachute,
stumbles over me. It is our last embrace.

(*CP*, 256)

The "guerilla warrior," who is, perhaps, an agent of the "democracy" that hunts the poet, kills him and dumps him into "ferns." Yet, after his death, the body of the poet continues to affect others. In this case, he causes the hero to stumble to his death ("It is our last embrace"). It is with this realization of the superiority of the serpent over the hero, as well as the realization of the serpent's ability to shape the "democracy" that hunts him, that O'Hara decides to "save the serpent."

In the final lines of the poem, O'Hara returns to the issue of his past selves, and states his decision to transform these past selves into art:

> And yet
> I have forgotten my loves, and chiefly that one, the cancerous
> statue which my body could no longer contain,
> against my will
> against my love
> become art,
> I could not change it into history
> and so remember it,
> and I have lost what is always and everywhere
> present, the scene of my selves, the occasion of these ruses,
> which I myself and singly must now kill
> and save the serpent in their midst.
>
> (*CP*, 257)

The "cancerous / statue which my body could no longer contain" is his past. As the Greeks in the third section left "the pain / at home to be converted into statuary," O'Hara himself must convert the pain of his own past into something else in order to deal with the pain of it. He could not, he writes, "change it into history." Therefore, he must metaphorically "kill" his past by placing it in a poem. The result is that he hopes to "save the serpent," or himself as a poet, rather than to construct some "coherent" self out of the multiple versions of himself.

This reading of the concluding lines of the poem offers a more consistent explanation of the words of the poem—in particular, that of "the serpent"—than the ones proposed by Perloff and Blasing. Both impose a concept of the self on O'Hara that is not his own. The self, for O'Hara, is a center of consciousness and exists to the extent that it feels itself in relation to other objects and other centers of consciousness. It is not, however, constituted by the presence of some objective, essential "something."[18] Furthermore, as is clear from poems such as *Second Avenue*, O'Hara was not concerned with rationalizing his experience and constructing some coherent whole out of instances of feeling. It is unlikely, therefore, that in "In Memory of My Feelings" O'Hara traces "the fragmentation and reintegration of the inner self" (*FOH*, 141).

It is also a reading that makes the most sense in light of what we know of the poem's own occasion. O'Hara began "In Memory of My Feelings" on what he thought was his thirtieth birthday. That night, Brad Gooch tells us, Grace Hartigan had a party for him (which is, perhaps, why he dedicated the poem to her). The event, however, was not an entirely happy one for O'Hara. Daisy Aldan, the editor of *Folder*, found him distressed and alone and asked him what was bothering him. "Because today I am thirty years old and have so little time left," he explained to Aldan, referring to the fact that Keats had achieved success as a poet at such a young age.[19] Later that night, O'Hara began "In Memory of My Feelings." The occasion of the poem then, seems to have been a concern that he had not accomplished what he wanted to accomplish in his work to date. "In Memory of My Feelings" is a poem in which O'Hara reflects on the personal value of art and determines to transform his experience into art and, therefore, both "be" and "accomplish" the work itself (*SS*, 17).

Finally, the present reading seems to make better sense of the form of the poem. As was noted at the beginning of the chapter, the self, for O'Hara, is a temporal form of the creative force of the universe. Some poets, according to O'Hara, have tended to see writing as a means of representing this creative force in a poem in a direct and absolute manner that, in the end, excludes the temporal manifestation of it in the actual person of the poet, or else they see writing as a means of representing the feelings of the poet in so much detail that the actual contents of the feelings of the poet are the poem. But "In Memory of My Feelings" can be understood as an effort to use personal details to express the creative force at work in the world in a manner that does not either elevate the personal details to the level of the poem or expunge them from the work itself. In this sense, it is perhaps related to Nietzsche's notion that great art must balance what he calls the "Apollonian" element ("the delimiting boundaries of the individual") and the "Dionysian" element ("the mysterious primordial unity") in the work itself.

5
Love

In this account of O'Hara's work, we have thus far focused on his view of artistic creation as an act of self-exploration that, in turn, renews our experience of the world. In "Memorial Day 1950," for example, O'Hara, rather than proposing some hidden alphabet of the human mind, places himself in relation to the European and American avant-garde and determines to explore his feelings in the medium of artistic creation in order to create artifacts that focus our attention on the passing, present material world, showing us that it is, indeed, "richer than a river." In poems such as *Second Avenue*, furthermore, O'Hara, while drawing from European surrealistic experiments, does not use automatism in order to locate some absolute form or essential structure of human experience. Rather, he explores the present moment in an effort to "muddy" language and, therefore, expand our experience of the world, which is, for O'Hara, in part mediated through language. In "In Memory of My Feelings," O'Hara shows that the self is both singular and multiple—both an expression of a constant creative force and a temporal form of one's accumulated aggregate experiences. It is a poem in which O'Hara reflects on the relationship between his singular self and his multiple selves and resolves to transform the individual moments of consciousness that constitute him into art. And in poems such as "A Step Away from Them" and "The Day Lady Died," O'Hara names moments and periods of experience to give them a temporal, concrete, and authentic form, that will reinvigorate his interest in and fascination with his present experience as well as renew past moments of feeling.

However, while O'Hara is preoccupied with the fleeting, momentary experience of the world in his poems, he is aware that this same preoccupation could lead him to ignore others. This concern is addressed in "Poem (The eager note on my door)" (1951). In this poem, the poet receives "an eager note" on his door, which states in a tone of desperation: " 'Call me, / call when you get in!' " (*CP*, 14). Rather than call, however, the poet throws "a few tangerines" into his "overnight bag" and heads "straight for the door" to visit his friend (*CP*, 14). Almost immediately he becomes distracted with his experience. The "leaves," he writes, "were brighter than grass on the sidewalk," and it is "autumn" by the time he gets "around the corner" (*CP*, 14). When he sees his friend's house, he seems to have forgotten the urgency of the note, and arrives as if by chance at a party:

> Funny, I thought, that the lights are on this late
> and the hall door open; still up at this hour, a
> champion jai-alai player like himself? Oh fie!
>
> (*CP*, 14)

When he enters his friend's apartment, he finds him dead. Thus, while the poem is somewhat humorous, it is also expresses O'Hara's awareness that his experience of the world—and, perhaps, art as well—can distract him from his responsibilities toward others.

While O'Hara has claimed on more than one occasion that the *impetus* to create must be always be internal (or personal) rather than external (or social), this does not mean that the completed work should not benefit others, or that the poet does not have certain responsibilities toward others in writing. This is evident, for example, in "Sleeping on the Wing" (1955). As James Schuyler notes, O'Hara wrote this poem in response to his and Joe LeSueur's teasing of O'Hara about his "unquenchable inspiration." As Schuyler explains later in Gooch's biography, the teasing consisted of an amicable challenge to O'Hara's seeming ability to write a poem at all times of the day and in all situations (*CP*, 536).[1] The theme of the poem he wrote in response is, in fact, "inspiration"—in particular, the implications of an inspiration that asks the poet to remove himself from everyday life and write in solitude. This is actually an inspiration that Schuyler and LeSueur are teasing O'Hara for *not* having. O'Hara begins the poem with a comparison between flying and writing and shows that flying, like writing, can separate the poet from the world:

> Perhaps it is to avoid some great sadness,
> as in a Restoration tragedy the hero cries "Sleep!
> O for a long sound sleep and so forget it!"
> that one flies, soaring above the shoreless city,
> veering upward from the pavement as a pigeon
> does when a car honks or a door slams, the door

of dreams, life perpetuated in parti-colored loves
and beautiful lies all in different languages.

Fear drops away too, like the cement, and you
are over the Atlantic. Where is Spain? Where is
who? The Civil War was fought to free the slaves,
was it? A sudden down-draught reminds you of gravity
and your position in respect to human love. But
here is where the gods are, speculating, bemused.
Once you are helpless, you are free, can you believe
that? Never to waken to the sad struggle of a face?
to travel always over some impersonal vastness,
to be out of, forever, neither in nor for!

(*CP*, 235)

O'Hara first compares flying to the escape of sleep. Flying separates one from the specific details of actual existence and the sadness that comes from one's experience of the metaphoric car honks and door slams. The farther one is above the earth, the more the harsher details of life lose clear definition. Thus, the ugliness and pain that come from one's experience of these specific details disappear and are replaced with a vague euphoria, where everything seems "beautiful" as one regards the "impersonal vastness" that the world has become.

O'Hara compares this detachment from the minute details of the world with theories of artistic creation that demand the poet separate himself from the world in order to create works that are impersonal and therefore objective. O'Hara grants that this understanding of artistic creation can, at first, be attractive to the artist. For, in separating himself from the world—and, in particular, other people (such as "the sad struggle of face" in the second section)—the artist removes himself from the sadness, fear, and pain that constitute life. He becomes one of the gods, "speculating" and "bemused." For O'Hara, this inhuman detachment is the danger in all theories of artistic creation where the artist separates himself from others.

The poet, however, experiences a "sudden down-draught," which reminds him of "gravity" and his "position in respect to human love." While the poet at first resists, at the end of the poem his sense of love for the world stirs his passion and sense of responsibility, and he returns to the earth (*CP*, 236). O'Hara writes:

And, swooping,
you relinquish all that you have made your own,

> the kingdom of your self sailing, for you must awake
> and breathe your warmth in this beloved image
>
> (*CP*, 236)

The "beloved image" in these lines is the world, which, a few lines earlier, O'Hara refers to as "an iceberg." Much of the world, O'Hara notes, is invisible. It lacks form and is cold, which, in turn, is a metaphor for sleep or death. Struck with a sense of longing or desire to return to the world and warm its cold form, the poet sacrifices his "kingdom" of self to "breathe" his "warmth" into the world and, therefore, shape its cold form, providing it with temporary "being." For O'Hara, then, love, whether it makes sense or not in his otherwise strict philosophical materialism, is a form of inspiration, as it was for Pasternak, in whose work the poet is possessed with both a desire and a sense of duty to return to the world, even if this means returning to the sadness and pain of the world in order to breathe momentary life into it.[2]

As it will be shown, however, in addition to being a metaphor for the poet's impetus to create, love is, for O'Hara, one of the noblest emotions. He explores this in detail in a number of his later poems, and in particular in his collection *Love Poems (Tentative Title)* (1965). In these poems, O'Hara defines love as the chance coming together of two people. One of the ironies of this is that while love is, for O'Hara, a feeling that is the result of movement, or the unexpected coming together of two otherwise separate entities, and is itself characterized as a moving, "life-giving vulgarity," it produces a feeling of peace and stillness—a feeling that will not remain, because of the fact that the self changes and that love is itself a moving, living thing. Thus, love contains within itself the ominous promise of future loss and is, therefore, both noble and vicious, the highest feeling that contains within itself the seeds of the lowest.

Love as Metaphor

The first thing to note concerning the notion of love in O'Hara's poems is that it is a metaphor for the act of creation itself. Following the example of both Rilke and Pasternak, O'Hara understands the poet's renewal of our awareness of the forgotten and even "turgid" things of the world to be an act of love in that the poet provides these things with a new "being." That O'Hara understood artistic creation to be a form of directing our attention toward the material world and, therefore, as an expression of love, rather than a form of rationalizing the material world, is clear in "Poem (If I knew exactly why the chestnut tree)" (1951). O'Hara writes:

> If I knew exactly why the chestnut tree
> seems about to flame or die, its pyramids
>
> aquiver, would I tell you? Perhaps not.
> We must keep interested in foreign stamps,
>
> railway schedules, baseball scores, and
> abnormal psychology, or all is lost. I
>
> could tell you too much for either of us
> to bear, and I suppose you might answer
>
> in kind. It is a terrible thing to feel
> like a picnicker who has forgotten his lunch.
>
> (*CP*, 40–41)

O'Hara compares the change that takes place in the natural world in the seasons with the changing, man-made "objects," such as foreign stamps, // railway schedules, baseball scores, and / abnormal psychology." The change that the poet observes in the tree is an example of the change that takes place throughout the material world and, in particular, the change that death causes. He could explain both why the tree changes and other things that would be "too much for either of us / to bear," he says, but this is why he does not. A further reason for his decision not to tell us "why the chestnut tree / seems about to flame or die" is that such an explanation would distract us from the beauty of the tree itself. This is evoked in the image of the picnicker, who, preoccupied with his forgotten lunch, is unable to enjoy either his natural surroundings or the picnic itself:

> And everything will take care of itself,
> it got along without us before. But god
>
> did it all then! And now it's our tree
> going up in flames, still blossoming, as if
>
> it had nothing better to do! Don't we have
> a duty to it, as if it were a gold mine

> we fell into climbing desert mountains,
> or a dirty child, or a fatal abscess?
>
> (*CP*, 41)

The "duty" that O'Hara feels for the tree in these lines is not to save it from changing colors, which O'Hara figures as "going up in flames" (*CP*, 41). Rather, like the tree, which has "nothing better to do," the poet asks us, it seems, to direct our attention toward it and register its change. For the tree will change colors whether we can make sense of it or not, and the great danger is that in trying to make sense of it, we may not experience the tree's change at all, which is the sole solace available to us in what would otherwise be a moment of total loss.

O'Hara refers to his "duty" to the changing world on a number of occasions in his poems. In "Meditations in an Emergency" (1954), which was originally titled "Meditations on Re-emergent Occasions," O'Hara, after losing another lover (hence, the "re-emergent occasions" in the original title), reflects on the nature of his ex-lover's commitment to him and his own commitment to the material world (*CP*, 532). While he faults his lover for his lack of commitment to what he calls his "restless" and changing self, he asks if he himself has not failed the changing world as his lover has failed him.

At the beginning of the poem O'Hara introduces the fact that his lover has left him and notes his sense of hurt at his lover's lack of commitment to him:

> Am I to become profligate as if I were blond? Or religious as if I were French?
>
> Each time my heart is broken it makes me feel more adventurous (and how the same names keep recurring on that interminable list!), but one of these days there'll be nothing left with which to venture forth.
>
> Why should I share you? Why don't you get rid of someone else for a change?
>
> I am the least difficult of men. All I want is boundless love.
>
> Even trees understand me! Good heavens, I lie under them, too, don't I? I'm just like a pile of leaves.
>
> (*CP*, 197)

While O'Hara claims he feels "more adventurous," his subsequent remark that his lover's rejection of him will exhaust him, thus making him celibate or "religious," expresses the clear sense of loss the poet feels at what is presented as but one more rejection. His humorous and ironic remark that he is "the least difficult of men" because all he needs is "boundless love," however, serves to introduce O'Hara's central complaint against his lover. While the term "boundless," of course, means "vast," which is how O'Hara uses it here, it can also mean "without limits." In this second sense, O'Hara's need for "boundless love" could be understood to refer to his need for a love that is not monogamous, which makes "getting rid" of someone—in this case, O'Hara—unneeded. His lover, however, has "misunderstood" O'Hara's needs and O'Hara's definition of love, and chooses between O'Hara and someone else.

Following this, O'Hara draws an implicit comparison between the lack of commitment of his partner to his "fleeting" self and his own commitment to the ever-changing material world in his poems. What O'Hara notes is that his love of the material world—unlike, perhaps, his ex-lover's love for him—is one of self-sacrificial attention toward the unseemly, or unlovable, (mostly man-made) objects. He writes:

> However, I have never clogged myself with the praises of pastoral life, nor with nostalgia for an innocent past of perverted acts in pastures. No. One need never leave the confines of New York to get all the greenery one wishes—I can't even enjoy a blade of grass unless I know there's a subway handy, or a record store or some other sign that people do not totally *regret* life. It is more important to affirm the least sincere; the clouds get enough attention as it is and even they continue to pass. Do they know what they're missing? Uh huh.
> (*CP*, 197)

Here O'Hara determines that the objects of his poetic affection will not be those common objects of poetic affection, such as "pastoral life" or "clouds," but things that seem inappropriate as vehicles of so-called poetic sentiments. With the use of the word "sincere," and its denotative meaning of "genuine" or "unadulterated," O'Hara draws attention to the fact that to treat certain aspects of the natural world—"the clouds" for instance—as "pure" is a creative act of the mind rather than mere description. Clouds are no more "pure" or "sincere" than dirt; however, because poets have been preoccupied with certain aspects of the material world such as clouds to the exclusion of other parts of it, which O'Hara views as unethical, he states his intention here to focus on those ignored aspects—the so-called least sincere things—to show that these are indeed no less or no more "pure" than the clouds themselves.

With the next section, however, O'Hara draws an implicit comparison between his love of the material world and his ex-lover's lack of love for him. He writes:

> My eyes are vague blue, like the sky, and change all the time; they are indiscriminate but fleeting, entirely specific and disloyal, so that no one trusts me. I am always looking away. Or again at something after it has given me up. It makes me restless and that makes me unhappy, but I cannot keep them still. If only I had grey, green, black, brown, yellow eyes; I would stay at home and do something. It's not that I'm curious. On the contrary, I am bored but it's my duty to be attentive, I am needed by things as the sky must be above the earth. And lately, so great has *their* anxiety become, I can spare myself little sleep.
>
> (*CP*, 197)

On the one hand, O'Hara, too, seems to be "passing," ever-changing, like the clouds. His eyes "change all the time" and are "fleeting," which, in turn, is a cause of unhappiness for him, as it is for the clouds in the previous section that "miss" the attention of the poet. O'Hara here communicates to his ex-lover his sense of loss at his own lack of commitment and attention. On the other hand, it is important to note that it is not O'Hara's self that changes in this passage, even if such a view is implied, but the object of the poet's attention. Unlike his ex-lover's love, which is "bound" to particular people and, therefore, excludes others, O'Hara's love of the material world figured in his constant looking is "indiscriminate" and vast. This constant and ever-changing focus of attention is something that does not make him happy, but he chooses to give his attention nonetheless, thus figuring his love of the material as self-sacrificial and dutiful. The love of his ex-lover, it is implied, is self-serving. It is unclear whether O'Hara can in fact make sense of such a notion, given his otherwise strict philosophical materialism; but in any case love is defined as a self-sacrificial giving of one's attention to other people and things. O'Hara thereby parallels John Donne in *Devotions on Emergent Occasions* (1624), another possible source of the poem's title, when Donne writes that the fear of losing one's life "shall seeme love, a love of having, and it is but a feare, a jealous, suspitious feare of losing," and Rilke when he remarks in *Letters to a Young Poet* (1934),

> If you will cling to Nature, to the simple in Nature, to the little things that hardly anyone sees, and that can so unexpectedly become big and beyond

> measuring; if you have this love of inconsiderable things and seek quite simply, as one who serves, to win the confidence of what seems poor: then everything will become easier, more coherent and somehow more conciliatory for you, not in your intellect, perhaps, which lags marveling behind, but in your inmost consciousness, waking and cognizance.[3]

Rilke claims here that a self-sacrificial love of the "inconsiderable things" in nature will, in the end, serve the poet on the long run, in particular in making things "more coherent and somehow more conciliatory."

Toward the end of the poem, however, O'Hara questions whether he has to be dutiful in his "love" of the material world, and, in addition to this, whether his "love" of the material world will transform these "turgid" objects of his poetic attention into vehicles of beauty and wonder. He wraps himself, therefore, in "the robes" of St. Serapion, but, in the end, does not come to a conclusion regarding his ability to love the material world in this self-sacrificial manner in his poems, or continue to plead his case with his ex-lover. He writes:

> I've got to get out of here. I choose a piece of shawl and my dirtiest suntans.
> I'll be back, I'll re-emerge, defeated, from the valley; you don't want me to go
> where you go, so I go where you don't want me to. It's only afternoon, there's
> a lot ahead. There won't be any mail downstairs. Turning, I spit in the lock
> and the knob turns.
>
> (*CP*, 198)

While O'Hara claims that he will "re-emerge," thus seemingly reversing the reemergent occasion of losing lovers, this reemergence at the end of the poem is not a victorious moment but a "defeated" one. One way of making sense of this is to take the word "defeated" to refer not to the poet's defeated artistic will to create, but to his "defeated" love. Thus, these lines point to the poet's resolve to continue to reemerge from defeated loves and even defeated experiments in art, to continue to love and to write despite the pain it brings. This decision to continue is itself a victory—and perhaps the sole victory available to the contemporary poet or artist.

These final lines, however, remain ambiguous. Part of the reason is that there is a conflict throughout "Meditations in an Emergency," as well as in the poem written the week before, "Ode (An idea of justice may be precious)" (1954), between O'Hara's notion of love as a self-sacrificial duty and his sense of jealous loss at his lover's decision to leave him. In the final lines of "Meditations in an Emergency," for example, while the poet resolves to move forward with his life, his determination to do so is emptied of its force by the poet's desire to remain with the person who has rejected him. The poet needs "to get out of here," but promises before he even leaves that he will "be back," not victorious in the arms of another lover, but "defeated." Furthermore, in an ironic act of defiance and independence, the poet promises to go where his lover does not want him to go (which is, of course, *with* him), and while the poet claims that there is "a lot ahead," his sense of isolation and loneliness figured in his lack of mail undercuts this optimistic claim. Finally, while the poet's spit could be understood to be the cause of the doorknob turning, one could take it to refer to either the ex-lover's return or the poet's hope of such a return. If this is the case, there is a tension in these final lines where O'Hara's sense of loss, and his jealous demand that the lover "get rid of someone else for a / change," is shown to be self-pleasing in its motive, and, therefore, lacking in the very love O'Hara criticizes his lover for not having. The poet is aware that he must move on in order to continue to be "the Lover of the quick world," as O'Hara puts in "The Satyr" (1951), but that means he must give up the very hope he does not want to give up—that his lover will, indeed, return to him (*CP*, 68). This, it seems, is the "trap" that has been set for O'Hara, and it is a trap that we come across again and again in his love poems.

Love Poems

Love, for O'Hara is more than a mere metaphor for the artist's creative act. It is also one of the noblest emotions. For O'Hara, emotive love is not something that is willed, but something that happens to someone. It is the chance converging of two entities (which, in turn, is the result of the world's constant motion) that makes love both an amazing occurrence and one that is always temporal. This is evident in "Poem V (F) W" (1959), which is the lead poem in *Love Poems (Tentative Title)*. The poem is addressed to Vincent Warren, with whom O'Hara had a relationship at the time. After establishing the fact that he is "independent of the Cabaret Voltaire / the Café Grinzing and the Black Cat," O'Hara recounts a moment when he saw Warren but at first did not recognize him:

> you were walking down a street softened by rain
> and your footsteps were quiet

and I came around the corner
inside the room
to close the window
and thought what a beautiful person
and it was you
no I was coming out of the door
and you looked sad
which you later said was tired
and I was glad
you had wanted to see me
and we went forward
back to my room
to be alone in your mysterious look

(*CP*, 347)

The situation of O'Hara's chance meeting with Warren is set against what might best be described as a nexus of moving planes and lines. Warren is moving forward on the street outside when O'Hara, who is in his apartment, is moving inside the room perpendicular to the street to close the window and sees Warren below on the sidewalk. The lack of recognition, followed by the realization that it is in fact Warren, is an experience that, O'Hara notes, is akin to the surprise or the unpredictable nature of emotive love.

The fact that O'Hara corrects the facts of his chance observation of Warren, however, points to the fragile nature of love. In what follows, O'Hara and Warren's movement in opposite directions—O'Hara is leaving the apartment and Warren is entering the apartment—is a metaphor for the movement of each mind, which, as O'Hara notes in the preceding section of the poem, seem not to meet at times ("two parallel lines always meet / except mentally"). Tragedy, however, is avoided as O'Hara's misreading of Warren's mood ("sad") is corrected ("tired") and O'Hara finds himself "glad" that Warren in fact wants to see him. Both, therefore, move "forward" together "back" to O'Hara's room, to be "alone." Thus, the two converge. However, what O'Hara points to here is that while the unpredictable nature of emotive love is the root source of what makes it such an exhilarating experience, it is also what makes it so fragile. If love is the chance coming together of two entities—a coming together that, as O'Hara explores elsewhere, is perhaps always temporal because of the fact that the world and the self are subject to constant change—then there is no assurance that chance might not pull them apart again.

In "Avenue A" (1960), O'Hara evokes the notion that the feeling of love is part and parcel of its unpredictable occurrence. Here the sudden appearance of the moon strikes him as all the more beautiful because after many years in the city he has been unaccustomed to looking at it:

> We hardly ever see the moon any more
> so no wonder
> it's so beautiful when we look up suddenly
> and there it is gliding broken-faced over the bridges
> (*CP*, 355–56)

The feeling that O'Hara has as he looks at the moon is related to the feeling that he has as he looks at Warren, whose face, like the moon, "is more mysterious than spring, the El Greco / heavens breaking open and then reassembling like lions / in a vast tragic veldt" (*CP*, 356). With this comparison, however, comes the realization that like his passing experience of the moon, his love for Warren, or Warren's love for him, may prove to be equally as passing. Indeed, O'Hara refers to their passion for each as "temporally united" (*CP*, 356). However, while O'Hara perhaps foresees the end of his and Warren's relationship, he decides to live in the moment and not allow the possible future to distract him from the present. He concludes:

> these are my delicate and caressing poems
> I suppose there will be more of those others to come, as in the past
> so many!
> but for now the moon is revealing itself like a pearl
> to my equally naked heart
> (*CP*, 356)

In the end, O'Hara's sense here that his relationship with Warren would soon be over proved true; and while the "other" poems were written—poems that lament the poet's sense of alienation from others and the world—O'Hara continued to have the same high view of love. Indeed, for all the emphasis on O'Hara's relationship to the visual arts, few critics have noted O'Hara's belief that love is higher than art—that it can render art (at least O'Hara's conception of art) superfluous. This is perhaps nowhere clearer than in "Having a Coke with You" (1960). In this poem, O'Hara compares works of art with the love embodied in the person of Vincent Warren. He notes that art, while an embodiment of love for the natural world, is, in the end, somehow less alive when compared to the present love that he feels for Warren. He writes:

> it is hard to believe when I'm with you that there can be anything as still
> as solemn as unpleasantly definitive as statuary when right in front of it
> in the warm New York 4 o'clock light we are drifting back and forth
> between each other like a tree breathing through its spectacles
>
> and the portrait show seems to have no faces in it at all, just paint
> you suddenly wonder why in the world anyone ever did them
> I look
> at you and I would rather look at you than all the portraits in the world
> except possibly for the *Polish Rider* occasionally and anyway it's in the Frick
> which thank heavens you haven't gone to yet so we can go together the first time
> and the fact that you move so beautifully more or less takes care of Futurism
> just as at home I never think of the *Nude Descending a Staircase* or
> at a rehearsal a single drawing of Leonardo or Michelangelo that used to wow me
> and what good does all the research of the Impressionists do them
> when they never got the right person to stand near the tree when the sun sank
> or for that matter Marino Marini when he didn't pick the rider as carefully
> as the horse
> it seems they were all cheated of some marvelous experience
> which is not going to go wasted on me which is why I'm telling you about it
> (*CP*, 360)

As striking as the art is, O'Hara notes here that it is seems temporarily "dead" when compared with love and life. The definitiveness of "statuary" is contrasted with the movement of "drifting back and forth" that characterizes O'Hara and Warren's love. Here, the stillness of the "statuary" evokes the thought of death and is, therefore, tagged unpleasant. The portraits, furthermore, seem to lack the detail that is supposed to characterize such pieces when compared to the living face of Warren. Warren's naked body renders *Nude Descending a Staircase* superfluous, and his unadorned bodily movements at dance practice produce an exhilaration that futurism, despite its elevated hope in technological advances, failed to produce. Thus, the presence of Warren and the attachment O'Hara feels for him are presented here as an experience that supersedes, at least momentarily, his experience of great works of art.

O'Hara expressed this high view of love on a number of occasions. For example, in "A Hill" (1954), O'Hara writes:

Yes, but don't be
scared; poetry
is intangible and
there's no purity

in me
outside of love,
which you can easily wreck
            and I can lose.

(*CP*, 204)

The idea that "love" is the sole thing that is pure, even if its presence is precarious, is expressed in O'Hara's "Statement for *The New American Poetry*," where he writes, as was noted in chapter 1, "I would rather die for love, but I haven't" (*CP*, 500). The humor of this sentence aside, O'Hara expresses here his firm belief that love is indeed superior to and more noble than art.

Yet love is also problematic for O'Hara. For one thing, when his need for love is not met, the poet is often unable to find pleasure in his present experience of the world. In "Poem (Although I am a half hour)" (1951), for example, when the poet arrives home "a half hour / early" in order to be sure not to miss meeting whomever he had planned to meet, he finds the apartment empty. He writes:

I am alone now. Only
my own face stares back
from the window, the
record, this white paper.

I put on my black shirt
and my sneakers, whistle
Glazounoff and try to
pick up the dirty room.

Last night I said "I'm
sick." Today is very windy.
The curtains are pulled
back but the sun goes

somewhere else. I've
seen all the movies. I
think I'm going to cry.
Yes. To kill the time.

(*CP*, 40)

The poet's disappointment creates a situation where he finds himself experiencing the present as banal and dark rather than as a moment of pleasure. While the poem is both a record of his black mood and an effort to connect imaginatively with whoever is not there, it becomes itself a part of an effort to "kill the time."

Another problem, as Alan Feldman has pointed out, is that love presents itself in opposition to the self. The self is always changing in O'Hara's work, and it makes him "regret change."[4] In "Poem (A la recherche d' Gertrude Stein)" (1959), for example, love provides the poet with a sense of strength and confidence in front of life's "enemies":

> when I am in your presence I feel life is strong
> and will defeat all its enemies and all of mine
> and all of yours and yours in you and mine in me
> sick logic and feeble reasoning are cured
> by the perfect symmetry of your arms and legs
> spread out making an eternal circle together
> creating a golden pillar beside the Atlantic
> the faint line of hair dividing your torso
> gives my mind rest and emotions their release
> into the infinite air where since once we are
> together we always will be in this life come what may
>
> (*CP*, 349)

While the presence of Vincent provides his ever-changing feelings and self with rest and meaning, the knowledge that this love will not, in fact, remain forever pushes the poet to find an argument—in this case, he paraphrases Gertrude Stein and writes, "[A] thing continues to exist in the time of its happening even though other things happen before or later"—in order to allay his discontentment at this fact (*CP*, 546).

However, while love will not in fact remain, in the end O'Hara seems to echo Alfred Lord Tennyson's famous quotation of Augustine of Hippo in the twenty-seventh elegy of *In Memoriam* (1850) that it is "better to have loved and lost / Than never to have loved at all."[5] For O'Hara, even in its tentative, temporal manifestations, love is something that has the power to transform the occasions in which it manifests itself. In "Poem (Light clarity avocado salad in the morning)" (1959), love "changes everything like a chemical dropped on a paper / and all thoughts disappear in a strange quiet excitement," and in

"Sudden Snow," O'Hara describes love as "like a path in the snow we are making / though no one else can follow, leading us only / to the ocean's sure embrace of summer, serious and free" (*CP*, 350, 355). While the poet may lose love, as he notes in "A Hill," it is an experience that is worth whatever pain it causes at its loss.

Conclusion: After O'Hara

THE FINAL POEM OF *THE COLLECTED POEMS OF FRANK O'HARA* IS "Little Elegy for Antonio Machado" (1966). It is slightly ironic that this should be one of O'Hara's last poems (it was dated March 27, 1966—three months before O'Hara's own death), given that Machado's own last lines were found a few days after his death in 1939, scrawled on a piece of paper in his overcoat.[1] Donald Allen notes that a shortened version of the poem first appeared in John Myers's show, "Homage to Machado," which Myers organized to benefit refugees from Spain (*CP*, 557). In the poem, O'Hara evaluates Machado's significance and praises him in terms that can be applied to O'Hara's own work.

The poem opens with the argument that while Machado himself is dead, he continues to be an active agent in the world though his poems:

> Now your protesting demons summon themselves
>   with fire against the Castilian dark
> and solitary light
>   your mother dead on the hearth
> and your heart at rest on the border of constellary futures
>
> no domesticated cemeteries can enshroud your flight
>   of linear solarities and quiescent tumbrils
> vision of the carrion
>   past made glassy and golden
> to reveal the dark, the dark in all its ancestral clarity
>
> (*CP*, 491)

While the poet himself is silent, his poems continue to please our senses with flights "of linear solarities and quiescent tumbrils" and shape our view of the present world by summoning his "protesting demons" to show us that we live in darkness. Thus, the poet himself is neither fully present nor fully absent. He is "at rest," but not in "domesticated cemeteries"; instead, he inhabits a point that seems to be outside of time, "on the border of constellary futures."

Darkness, in Machado's poems, is most often a symbol of death and destruction, and light, a symbol of new life. In *Campos de Castilla* (1907–17), to which O'Hara alludes in these lines, Machado contrasts images of ancient Castile with those of modern Spain to argue that the present is characterized by decay. This is what O'Hara seems to refer to when he writes that in Machado's work the past is made "glassy and golden" to show the present to be "dark." That this past is "carrion," according to O'Hara—which is to say, dead and decomposing—underscores the fact that it is Machado's work that *makes* it "glassy and golden." O'Hara's reference to Machado's work as a form of fire is important in this respect. On the one hand, it is the hot hearth out of which molded artifacts—in this case, images of the past—emerge "glassy and golden." On the other hand, it is a destructive force. It consumes the carcasses of the "carrion past" and molds them into something new. This consumption, furthermore, is not carried out with passionless disinterestedness. After all, according to O'Hara, Machado summons his "demons" in the same way as Satan passionately summons his army of demons in book 1 of Milton's *Paradise Lost* (1667) against the darkness of hell, and who, in turn, respond with protests. Thus, O'Hara figures Machado's act of creation as both an act of construction and destruction.

In addition to this, O'Hara alludes to Machado's ambiguous use of the images of light and darkness in his poems. As Norma Louise Hutman notes, Machado believes in the cyclical nature of time and in the interconnectedness of all things, and in his poems images of light and darkness can come to symbolize the absent other. While darkness symbolizes death and destruction, it points to a future dawn; and while light symbolizes life, it points to an inevitable future darkness.[2] O'Hara highlights this same interconnectedness in his use of the word "dark." For example, while the phrase "dark in all its ancestral clarity" refers to Machado's use of the "golden" past to show the present to be in darkness, O'Hara makes "clarity," one of the common attributes of light, an attribute of darkness. This underscores the interconnected meaning of both terms.

In the third and fourth sections of the poem, O'Hara turns to another common image of Machado's: water. O'Hara writes:

> where our futures lie increasingly in fire
>   twisted ropes of sound encrusting our brains
> your water air and earth
>   insist on our joining you
> in recognition of colder prides and less negotiable ambitions

we shall continue to correct all classical revisions
    of ourselves as trials of ceremonial worth
and purple excess
        improving your soul's expansion
in the night and developing our own in salt-like praise

(*CP*, 491)

The vaguely ominous "fire" of the third section, which is different from the fire in the first, is cooled, according to O'Hara, by Machado's "water air and earth." These images most often represent finite experience in Machado's work. While it is unclear what these "colder prides and less negotiable ambitions" are that Machado's "water air and earth" insist we recognize, O'Hara's reference to "classical revisions / of ourselves" later in the same section as "trials of ceremonial worth" rather than as actual worth invites comparisons to the work of the French symbolist poet Jean Moréas, whom Machado met in Paris in 1899.[3] As a symbolist poet, Moréas was, indeed, ambitious. As he stated in his symbolist manifesto in *Le Figaro* in 1886, "[S]ymbolic poetry works to clothe the Idea in sensible form" [la poésie symbolique cherche à vêtir l'Idée d'une forme sensible].[4] While Moréas argues that this sensible form is often ambiguous or mysterious because of its relationship to "the Idea," concrete descriptions of the material world, such as one finds in Machado's work, are scorned.[5] Moréas would later distance himself from symbolism, but he continued to understand poetry as clothing "the Idea" in sensible form, and drew from classical texts in his later work, such as in *Les stances* (1899–1901).[6] In contrast to the confident, Neoplatonic poems of Moréas, Machado's poems are tentative, often ending in uncertainty. As Hutman notes: "Water is the flow of the river to soundless sea and the source of life; roads signify our mortal existence and also continuity; nature is reborn and man may therefore hope—but never with certainty of fulfillment—also to be reborn."[7]

This does not mean, however, that Machado's poems are no longer concerned with meaning. Rather, while Machado, according to O'Hara, continues to be involved with questions of meaning in his poems, it is not the propositional content of these "classical revisions" that is valuable, but rather the form created out of the process of correction. This is the reason that O'Hara refers to this continual revision of ourselves as a trial of "ceremonial worth" as opposed to actual worth—one that is furthermore characterized as an example of "purple excess." What is valuable, in other words, is the form left over from the search, the beauty of the ceremony itself long after the significance of the ceremony has been forgotten. According to O'Hara, therefore, Machado recognized rightly that "sensible form" alone (again in contradistinction to Moréas) is the principal end of poetry. It is because of this that all who follow Machado in this recognition, and here we can include O'Hara, will improve his or her "soul's expansion."

Whether or not Machado's work can be characterized as a commitment to a less ambitious view of poetic images and form, such a characterization can be applied to O'Hara's. Like painters such as Jackson Pollock, Willem de Kooning, and Robert Motherwell, and poets such as Walt Whitman and Boris Pasternak, O'Hara understands artistic creation as a form of expression. It is, for him, the process of exploring his feelings in the material elements of his medium. While O'Hara is aware of the fact that his feelings are inseparable from the words and forms he uses to express them, and he recognizes that there is an element of construction in all art, he does not espouse a reductive materialism that reduces all feelings to constructs. For O'Hara, artistic creation is a form of what Robert Motherwell calls "plastic automatism"—the exploration of the artist's or poet's feelings that come into being as the artist works in a particular medium—as well as an "intuitive craft."

Unlike a number of artists who understand artistic creation to be a form of expression, however, O'Hara thinks that these new forms do not provide us with some sort of insight regarding the nature of the force that provides form to the material world, including the self, and sustains it. In this sense, O'Hara has a much less ambitious, and more pragmatic, view of poetic form and images. This does not mean that poetry is no longer involved with questions of meaning; but for O'Hara the principal end of art is to reinvigorate our experience of the world. In his poems, therefore, O'Hara figures himself as "the Lover of the quick world"—a world that includes both "tree waves and thieves" and that is both comprehensible and incomprehensible (*CP*, 69). It is this view of the end of poetry—a view that is, indeed, more pragmatic and less ambitious—that most distinguishes O'Hara's work from the work of previous poets and the work of his contemporaries.

After his death in 1966, two groups of poets positioned themselves with respect to O'Hara—the so-called second generation of the New York School of Poets and the "L=A=N=G=U=A=G=E" poets. Both of these groups are indeed indebted to O'Hara. However, a close examination of their respective responses to O'Hara shows that each group oversimplifies O'Hara's poetics in certain respects. If Ted Berrigan (1934–83) is too quick to appropriate O'Hara's style and tone with little interest in the larger questions that inform O'Hara's poetics, Bob Perelman (b. 1947) and Charles Bernstein seem to respond to the poststructuralist version of O'Hara rather than to O'Hara himself. Somewhat surprisingly, poets such as David Shapiro (b. 1947) and James Tate (b. 1943), while not often associated with O'Hara, have a poetics that is much closer to O'Hara's than either of the above two groups.

The Second Generation of the "New York School of Poets"

According to Allen Ginsberg, St. Mark's Church-in-the-Bowery in New York's Lower East Side had been hosting poetry readings since at least the mid-1930s, when he first went there with his father, Louis, who was also a poet.[8] The Poetry Project at St. Mark's, however, did not begin until 1966, when Harry Silverstein, a sociologist at the New School for Social Research, applied for a grant from the Office of Economic Opportunity to work with youth from New York's Lower East Side.[9] A number of poets were already meeting at St. Mark's at the time to read their work, in particular Joel Oppenheimer and Paul Blackburn, who moved the reading series that took place at the Metro coffeehouse on Second Avenue to St. Mark's due to problems relating to free speech.[10] When the project started in 1966, Joel Oppenheimer was hired as the director of the project, and Anne Waldman (b. 1945) was hired as the assistant director.[11] Waldman served as the director of the project from 1968 to 1978. According to Waldman, Ted Berrigan served on the advisory board of the project, led a writing workshop, and was unofficial "bouncer" at the church, who "reasoned patiently and convincingly with the belligerent stray or drunk who reeled into the Parish Hall."[12] Ron Padgett (b. 1942) was also very involved. He founded the *Poetry Project Newsletter* and also served as the director of the project.[13]

While St. Mark's is often seen as being the center for a group of New York poets indebted to the example of O'Hara and Ashbery, the work of those associated with St. Mark's is very diverse. For example, in a number of important respects, Anne Waldman's early work is more related to Allen Ginsberg's *Howl* (1956) than it is to either O'Hara's or Ashbery's work. In her first books of poems, for example,

Fast Speaking Woman: Chants and Essays (1976), she draws from Ginsberg's use of repetition in the long title poem and in a great number of the shorter poems in the collection—hence the "Chants" in the subtitle. For Waldman, poetry is a kind of energy, and she associates this energy with the divine force that in Buddhism is said to underlie the material world. She writes in her essay, " 'I Is Another': Dissipative Structures," which appears at the end of *Fast Speaking Woman:* "Poetry is a kind of *siddhi* (Sanskrit for accomplishment) or energy. The poems that arrive for 'performance' (or those that have performance possibilities) seem to manifest psychological states of mind as well as states of energy. This is what attracts me so passionately to Vajrayana Buddhism, because this level of study and practice *engages* energy."[14]

This spiritualization of energy or power is one of the aspects of Waldman's work that shows it to be more related to that of Ginsberg and other so-called Beat poets. While the influence of O'Hara's later poems can nevertheless be seen in some isolated poems in the volume—such as "Talking Mushrooms"—the work is a product of California, not New York. While Waldman's second volume of poetry, *Journals and Dreams* (1976), which contains poems that are collages (as Waldman notes in the acknowledgments page) of phrases from her journals and travel writing, shows the influence of O'Hara and Ashbery in her use of disconnected phrases, her spacing, her personal and casual tone, and the integration of letters to friends and family members, overall the work continues Waldman's earlier investigation into what she calls "psychological states of mind" as manifestations of the divine energy at work in the world and in the self.

In the work of Berrigan and Padgett, the influence of O'Hara is much more evident. In 1964, Ted Berrigan published his first—and, as it would turn out, most original—book of poems, *The Sonnets.* While the influence of O'Hara is less present in *The Sonnets* than in later collections, such as in *Many Happy Returns* (1969) and *Train Ride* (1971 and 1978), a number of Berrigan's "sonnets" are nevertheless written almost entirely in the style of O'Hara's "I do this I do that" poems, while others imitate O'Hara's epistolary poems. Part of the reason that the style and diction of O'Hara's poems are so evident in *The Sonnets* is that Berrigan, according to Padgett, understood himself to be following the example of "found" art in the collages of Jean Arp (1886–1966), Marcel Duchamp (1887–1968), Max Ernst, and Tristan Tzara (1896–1963), as well as "the heroic example" of abstract expressionist "all-over" paintings. Padgett writes: "Ted had a license to operate in this no-holds-barred manner, a license granted by Duchamp, Tzara, Arp and Ernst (and later, Burroughs); particularly Duchamp, who was like a god to us. The heroic example of Abstract Expressionism (especially de Kooning, Pollock, and Hans Hofmann) was constantly before us, with each big and exciting and "all-over." And—to help tie it all together—hadn't Frank O'Hara written a book on Pollock?"[15] In his "book on Pollock," O'Hara remarks that both cubism and surrealism undermined the "post-Renaissance vision of visual structure supported by the rationalizations and syllogisms of semi-popular science" and, therefore, gained "greater liberation from the restrictions of preconceived form" and content (*AC*, 13). It is this liberation from "preconceived form" and content, Padgett seems to argue, that has granted Berrigan the "license" to use whatever material he wants in the creation of new artifacts.

The irony of needing a "license" to be free aside, while Berrigan is indeed indebted to O'Hara for the idea that one can include anything in a poem, no matter how corny or offensive, Berrigan's continued use of this freedom to create works that are, in the end, very similar to O'Hara's in terms of voice, style, and subject matter after *The Sonnets* is somewhat strange. As Libbie Rifkin has argued in her fascinating article on Berrigan's poetics in *Contemporary Literature:* "Like many of the poets in his cohort, Berrigan's formal experiments are best understood through their social aims and effects."[16] The main aim, for Berrigan, according to Rifkin, was to be *recognized* as a poet. This necessitated creating poems that, while original, embodied the accepted tenets of the particular group he hoped to join. Thus, in Berrigan, we have poetry that is written more in imitation of O'Hara's style than out of an engagement with O'Hara's poetics.

At times, Padgett too imitates O'Hara's style too closely. In his first individual book of poems, *Great Balls of Fire* (1969), a number of the poems are clearly indebted to O'Hara. In poems such as "Careless Ape," for example, Padgett draws from the spacing and the disconnected lines of O'Hara's later poems, and in "Words to Joe Ceravolo" Padgett follows O'Hara in his numerous epistolary poems. Padgett draws from O'Hara's rant poems in "You Again," and his odes, which are far less serious than O'Hara's odes, nevertheless evoke O'Hara's humorous use of logical fallacies and whimsical repartees.

However, while Padgett's work and much of his criticism is very much indebted to O'Hara, his interest in cubism distinguishes him from O'Hara in a number of important ways. For Padgett, artistic creation is primarily a form of construction. In his essay "Four French

Poets and the Cubist Painters" (1983), he defines the basic elements of "cubist" poetry. It contains, he writes, "a multiplicity of viewpoints (different planes in the same poem) and shifting voices (on the same plane)" and a "play on appearance and reality" in the use of "found materials and trompe l'oeil" as well as what Padgett calls 'trompe l'esprit.' "[17] Furthermore, it creates simultaneous meanings with "fragmented syntactical arrangements" and treats "everyday objects and occurrences (including dreams)" with what Padgett calls "a subdued palette."[18] The qualities of cubism that Padgett identifies in "Four French Poets and the Cubist Painters" can be found throughout his own work. In "16 November 1964," for example, Padgett recounts in a few lines of poetry the elements of his day. The poem serves as an example of Padgett's constructivist aesthetics. As he goes through his day, Padgett tells us, he encounters words and phrases that he writes down in a alphabetized "small blue notebook," which he carries with him "At all times, in case of emergencies."[19] As the poet comes across interesting phrases and words, he writes them down in his book:

> For example, the lady and her newspaper. She wanted
> To show me a headline which must have disturbed her,
> Because her hand trembled as she read to me, "FIREMEN CHOP
> THEIR WAY THROUGH SHED." I thanked the lady
> And started toward the stairs when I realized that
> The headline she had read me was rather astonishing.
> I went back inside and wrote it down.[20]

As he walks, he writes down the phrase "Do you realize that *they* are undermining your existence?" and later the phrase "Finger talk" after he meets a deaf mute who gives him a card.[21] He writes: " 'Who knows,' I said to myself, 'by the end of the day I may have written a poem!' "[22] The poem, therefore, is a narrative of Padgett's aesthetic of using "found" words to create a poem.

At the end of the poem, however, the poet opens his book to show us the four lines of poetry he has "written down during the day."[23] What is interesting here is that the lines do not correspond to the words or lines he found earlier in the poem. They are:

> This offers us the stale air of the balcony
> Of the future which you don't want or can,
> Blue, marigolds, the sum of all that you love in him,
> Where is it?[24]

On the one hand, these lines possess a number of further "cubist" qualities that Padgett notes in his essay on cubist poets. They create, for example, a number of simultaneous meanings through the use of "fragmented syntactical arrangements" and shifting voice. Everyday objects are named, but appear in a context that makes them seem strange and dreamlike. Furthermore, the fact that the words do not correspond to the lines "found" in the body of the poem corresponds to the element of surprise that one often finds in cubist paintings. The fact that the lines do not correspond to the lines "found" in the body of the poem, however, could also be understood to signal a break from cubist composition.

While it is unclear if this is how these lines should be read, there is no doubt from Padgett's other poems that cubism is an inspirational tool he uses to create poems. He does not use a cubist aesthetic out of an ethical interest to shape present values (though it is difficult to see how this could be avoided) but out of a desire, as he notes in "Four French Poets and the Cubist Painters," to create lines that are "lyrical, and continually fresh."[25] Thus, while Padgett differs from O'Hara in seeing poetic composition primarily in terms of cubist construction, he follows O'Hara in his understanding of the end of a poem. Furthermore, while Padgett's poems are perhaps less "continually fresh" than he would like, he nevertheless uses this constructivist paradigm to create poems that are less derivative, and, therefore, more interesting, than Berrigan's.

The "L=A=N=G=U=A=G=E" Poets

Drawing from the notion that poetic composition is a form of construction and poststructuralist theories of language, the so-called L=A=N=G=U=A=G=E poets, beginning in the early 1970s, positioned themselves with respect to O'Hara as well. Unlike Berrigan and Padgett's work, however, the work of these poets is very different from O'Hara's. These poets, beginning with Clark Coolidge (b. 1939), read O'Hara as a critic of poetic voice, who rejects meaning and self-expression in favor of the free play of linguistic signifiers. In "FO'H" Notes (1978), Coolidge writes:

> The secret is that flamboyance *can* be so exact. (discrete?) And the word "discreet" can be used for something more precise than prudence if you

> move one of those e's to that end. The feeling that he must have "talked" to himself (in mind) a lot, practicing up for those brightening placements on the perfectly flowing (swaying?) page. "you go on your nerve" And he's not afraid to include all-out rhapsody so that you titter but not out of embarrassment for his loss of possession. The lines can always be held entire. A pan-shot across gleaming NYC morning facades, which somehow stand for a completely different set of objects to be remembered, as in the mind of a mnemonist.[26]

Coolidge points to what he understands to be the constructed nature of O'Hara's seemingly "perfectly flowing" phrases and the feelings to which these phrases refer. His poems, Coolidge argues, are elaborate constructions that establish O'Hara's discreteness, or his individual voice. This voice, however, is not O'Hara's voice. While O'Hara often claimed that his work was the result of spontaneous enunciation—going on his "nerve"—and wrote, as Koch himself notes, seemingly without premeditation, Coolidge argues that "he must have 'talked' to himself (in mind) a lot"—hence, the numerous "perfectly flowing" phrases in his work.

To prove his point, Coolidge provides a number of such phrases that, in turn, seem to be constructed. Coolidge argues that O'Hara's phrases seem to precede the feeling contained in them. They are not immediate expressions of feeling spontaneously produced out of the poet's interaction with the world but rather carefully constructed lines. He uses words, Coolidge argues, to "inhabit certain points of the still world," and it is in this space that the poet's feelings are produced. Writing is thus a form of constructing a space in which, in the process of construction, the poet's feelings begin to inhabit that space; and therefore it is a form of "[r]ecording in awe of what's arriving, new to you who are speaking."[27]

Up until this point, Coolidge does not so much provide a basis for a "new materialist poetics" as he reformulates O'Hara's poetics in constructivist terms, pointing correctly to the fact that there is always an element of revision or planning in art no matter how seemingly spontaneous the final product. Yet, Coolidge's treatment of what he calls O'Hara's "loss of possession" in the more rhapsodic moments in his poems belies an uneasiness in Coolidge with respect to O'Hara's view of poetic voice as a form of "self-declaration" (*CP*, 310).[28] On two occasions in Coolidge's short creative piece, he refers to the possible embarrassment of O'Hara's rhapsodic moments in his poems, moments when O'Hara becomes preoccupied with his feelings to such an extent that he seems unaware of the fact that the construct of the poem is itself the cause of these feelings. In the section quoted above, for example, Coolidge writes, "[H]e's not afraid to include all-out rhapsody so that you titter," but is quick to add, "but not out of embarrassment for his loss of possession. The lines can always be held entire."[29] Furthermore, at the end of the piece, Coolidge writes: "His poems, almost embarrassingly these days (In Favor of One's Time), remind of the velocity of inspiration, or is it aspiration, everything following in its arrangement outward until it's all exhausted. A definite bonus that he never knows when to stop."[30] While Coolidge admits that O'Hara's preoccupation with his own feelings in his poems seems somewhat embarrassing, he tries to reassure his readers that this "velocity of inspiration" is staged.[31]

Following Coolidge, Charles Bernstein offers an explanation of what he calls Frank O'Hara's "achievement" in his essay "Stray Straws and Straw Men." It resides, Bernstein claims, in how O'Hara has "fronted" the notion of "naturalness."[32] For Bernstein, naturalness is the use of personal subject matter and a certain kind of syntax and diction that makes the events of the poem, and the "voice" of the poet, seem "authentic."[33] For Bernstein, however, there is no such thing as a "natural" or "authentic" language. These notions, he claims in "Three or Four Things I Know about Him," which is the opening piece of *Content's Dream* (1986), are the impositions of an "imperialistic" bourgeoisie that enforce things such as a "standardized spelling" and grammar as a means of enforcing a view of language as a representational tool, and, in turn, a view of the real world as "suprapersonal" and extralinguistic.[34] It is in removing language from the "participatory control of its users" that "the state" legitimizes capitalistic ideology as natural.[35] He writes:

> Imperial reality has as its essential claim not so much that it is *a* version of reality but that it is *the* version, i.e., (imperially) clear. That the composition of reality is suprapersonal: the mistakes & plain takes of a person are not an essential part of reality's composition. Standardized spelling, layout, & punctuation enter into a world of standardization—clocks & the orbit of the moon & the speed of light. A social science epistemologically self-conceived on the model of the natural sciences becomes possible & grammar becomes a social science. Language is thus removed from the participatory control of its users & delivered into the hands of the state.[36]

For Bernstein, "modern" poets have responded to the imposition of this supposed "suprapersonal" reality by reasserting the value of the "subjective" in various radical linguistic experiments. While subjectivity is defined in the current bourgeois state as that which is opposed to its version of the real world—as mere "fumbling clouds of vision that are to be dissolved by learning"— so-called modern artistic experiments (Bernstein refers to surrealism and the Beats) have defined "subjectivity in a sort of Nietzschean reversal, not as 'mere' but as exalted."[37] This, however, Bernstein claims, has not reversed subjectivity's marginalization, but, in some respects, provided justification for it by making the imposed ideological distinction between the objective real world and our subjective experience of it seem all the more natural.[38]

In "Stray Straws and Straw Men," Bernstein sees O'Hara's accomplishment as slightly above that of the surrealists and the Beats. For while O'Hara, too, is preoccupied with the events of his personal life in his poems, Bernstein notes that O'Hara's work "*proposes* a domain of the personal" and "not simply *assuming* it, fully works it out."[39] This, however, is not enough. What O'Hara fails to do, according to Bernstein, and what he implies he in fact accomplishes in his own work, is to show how personal feelings and poetic voice are always constructed. In the end, O'Hara does not "front" naturalness enough.[40]

While Bernstein argues that the constructed nature of experience must always be established in a poem, this does not mean, he claims, that the poem is always about the act of writing alone, or that the feelings or the events of the poem cannot be experienced as real. He writes: " 'But can I actually experience it?' Yes. But it reveals the conditions of its occurrence at the same time as it is experienced. So I don't feel a part of it as much as facing it. . . . Of course at times you forget. All of a sudden a few hours, a week, flash by before you actually notice, & you say to yourself 'how the time slips—[.]' "[41] In other words, for Bernstein, while one can experience the feelings or events of a poem as natural or real, such an experience necessitates that the reader "forget" that such feelings and events are constructed. Thus, the emotive effect of the poem is, in the end, dependent on the reader's suspension of disbelief.

Bob Perelman understands O'Hara's accomplishment in terms similar to those of Bernstein. In "A False Account of Talking with Frank O'Hara and Roland Barthes in Philadelphia," Perelman, following perhaps Ron Silliman's (b. 1946) criticism of Barthes's idealization of the reader (which, in turn, functions to replace the absent author in Barthes's hermeneutic), uses O'Hara to call into question Barthes's idealized reader, and Barthes to criticize what Perelman sees to be

O'Hara's failure to "front" (to borrow Bernstein's word) poetic voice.[42] While Perelman represents O'Hara as being aware of the constructed nature of poetic voice, he points to what he believes is O'Hara's failure to follow such a notion to its logical conclusions. For example, while Perelman, referring to "Personism," imagines O'Hara to state, "I hated poetic phrases," and has him scold Barthes for taking his use of the word "jolly" in "The Critic" (1951) literally. (He has O'Hara say, "Ah, Sir Roland, when I write it, you mustn't take 'jolly' to mean jolly. But perhaps your appetite for falseness was different from mine. All my words were as false as false eyelashes: but of course I'm looking directly at you when I say them.") But he depicts O'Hara as conflicted in his actual practice.[43] Furthermore, when Perelman has O'Hara read "Heroic Sculpture" (1958), he presents him as somewhat embarrassed at the serious tone of the poem and its lack of "fronting": " 'Wait! How about this? We join the animals not when we fuck or shit not when tear falls but when staring into the light. . . .' O'Hara inserted a thin pause. ". . . we think. Oh, I don't know. I don't buy it myself. David Smith made me say it."[44]

The "thin pause," which provides the final lines with a serious, important tone, is something that O'Hara both likes and dislikes, and Perelman very humorously presents O'Hara as subject to losing "possession" of himself—to forgetting that the feelings presented in the poem are, in fact, constructs of the poem itself.[45]

Elsewhere, Perelman uses Barthes to call into question what Perelman believes to be O'Hara's uncritical understanding of poetic diction. For example, Barthes interrupts O'Hara's reading of "A Step Away from Them" with the remark: "Languorously agitating: Frank, I detect a poetic phrase—even an elaborately sounded structure."[46] O'Hara, preoccupied, misses the jibe. He responds: "It is nice, isn't it?" and continues reading. This, in the end, is Perelman's criticism of O'Hara. While Perelman understands O'Hara to be aware of the constructed nature of poetic diction, he was unable to follow those presuppositions to their logical conclusions. "That's why" Perelman states in his own voice and with a bit of self-aggrandizement, "neither of you were language writers."[47]

As interesting as it is, this implicit identification of O'Hara by Bernstein and Perelman as a forerunner of their own poetics is, it seems to me, based on a misunderstanding of his work. Both Bernstein and Perelman take certain statements in O'Hara's work—statements such as "the clear architecture of the nerves" and his remarks on mechanics in "Personism"—as pointing to a poststructuralist understanding of feeling and the self as constructed. Yet, such an understanding of O'Hara's poetics does not square with O'Hara's view of artistic creation as a form of expression and his understanding of poetry as a form of "self-declaration" in addition to its being a form of reinvigorating our experience of the world (*CP*, 310).

O'Hara is aware of the fact that artistic creation is always, to some extent, a form of construction. In "Post the Lake Poets Ballad" (1959), for example, in which O'Hara responds to Larry Rivers's letter accusing him of "gorgeous self-pity," O'Hara writes:

> that is odd I think of myself
> as a cheerful type who pretends to
> be hurt to get a little depth into
>   things that interest me
>
> and I've even given that up
> lately with the stream of events
> going so fast and the movingly
>   alternating with the amusingly
>
> (*CP*, 336)

Rather than dramatized self-pity, which, it seems, is what Rivers refers to with the adjective "gorgeous," O'Hara argues that while his poems are indeed full of staged hurts, he uses them not as an end in themselves, but to add emotional weight to "things that interest" him. The fact that the title of the poem evokes the *Lyrical Ballads* (1798) underscores O'Hara's point that the moments of feelings in his poems are, at least in part, staged, though not, he hopes, melodramatic. It is interesting to note, however, that in the second section O'Hara turns and claims to have even given up such staging because of the speed of life. He does not have the time, he claims, to stage, much less dramatize, self-pity. The best he can do, he implies, is transcribe "the movingly / alternating with the amusingly" (*CP*, 336). The "movingly" and "amusingly" are instances of experience that exists at the moment of the self's contact with the world and are the "facts" of the self prior to the poet's naming of them; and it is this effort to name them—an effort that O'Hara viewed as always imperfect and temporal—that poetry is, in addition to a form of reinvigorating our experience of the world, a form and a never-ending testament of the self.

In this connection, Kenneth Koch's evaluation of O'Hara's accomplishment seems to be the most accurate. In "All the Imagination Can Hold (*The Collected Poems of Frank O'Hara*)," Koch writes:

> Frank O'Hara's work has already influenced a generation of younger poets; some of those who are not poets may find it hard to judge the importance of what he has done when critics so often mistake solemnity for seriousness, obscurity for profundity, and the expression of pain for intensity of feeling. O'Hara's poems are buoyant, exuberant, wild, personal, open in troubling and troublesome ways, sometimes humorous, often about seemingly ordinary or trivial things, and radically original in form. They are the result of an unfamiliar aesthetic assumption: that what is really there, in the poet's thoughts, fantasies, and feelings, is what is richest in possibility and worth the most attention.[48]

What Koch points to here is that O'Hara's valuing of actual feelings and not mere mechanical innovation is what makes his work so valuable. Responding in many ways to the L=A=N=G=U=A=G=E poets' criticism before that criticism had even been formulated, Koch continues: "In a book of twenty or thirty poems, certain of Frank O'Hara's subjects (lunch, movies) could seem trivial and willful because chosen at the expense of others; in this book of five hundred poems what strikes one is the breadth, sincerity, and exuberance of his concern for life. At first overwhelming, it is also liberating: by caring so much for so many things, he gives us back feelings of our own and permits us to respect them."[49]

It is important to note that Koch does not reject the notion that O'Hara's poems create feelings; however, O'Hara does not restrict his poems, as Bernstein does his, for example, to nothing but this notion. Noting the fact that O'Hara wrote quickly in order to capture a feeling "while it [was] really there and still taking place," Koch writes: "There is a difference between a feeling seized rapidly, while it's happening, or while it's being created (for his poems create feelings as much as they expose them) and feeling considered in any other way. In catching a feeling in the process of coming into being, or as it first explodes into a thousand refractions, one can hope to reveal some of the truth that lies hidden in our unconscious, in all the things we have known and felt but can't be aware of simultaneously."[50] While Koch is too quick to take O'Hara's claim at face value and is incorrect to claim that O'Hara was concerned with discovering some hidden "truth" in the unconscious, it is true that the expression of his feelings in his poems does indeed propose certain truths about the world—the principal one being, as Koch himself notes at the outset of his review, that feelings are the irreducible building blocks of the self.[51]

His reading, therefore, of poems such as "Easter" and *Second Avenue* differs from that of later critics in his understanding that these poems were far from mere constructs or confections. Noting that "Easter" "burst on us all like a bomb," Koch continues:

> I remember two things about it which were new: one was the phrase "the roses of Pennsylvania," and the other was the line in the middle of the poem which began "It is Easter!" . . . What I saw in these lines was 1) inspired irrelevance which turns out to be relevant (once Frank had said "It is Easter!" the whole poem was obviously about death and resurrection); 2) the use of movie techniques in poetry (in this case coming down hard on the title in the middle of a work); 3) the detachment of beautiful words from traditional contexts and putting them in curious new American ones ("roses of Pennsylvania").[52] Koch notes that the words O'Hara included in his poems were not so much constructions as they were names for O'Hara's passions and, thus, a form of affirming these passions as not trivial, but real.[53]

After the "L=A=N=G=U=A=G=E" Poets

Two poets that have followed O'Hara in his effort to use his personal experience of the world in his work to create poems that are, in turn, independent objects are David Shapiro and James Tate. As Thomas Fink points out in his excellent study of Shapiro's work, his poems are neither instances of seamless "confession" nor instances of mere formal play, but rather end products of a process of creation that are dependent upon (without being reduced to) the personal subject matter out of which they are created.[54] Fink writes: "In many of Shapiro's poems, one can interpret the use of what the Russian Formalists called 'de-familiarization' as a resistance to the degraded language of false collectivity (conformism) that characterizes much mass communication and the pronouncements of those in the American political establishment. The experimental poet creates a 'pocket' of freedom by expanding both the possibilities of personal expression and shared linguistic experience."[55] While Fink does not refer to O'Hara as a possible source of Shapiro's interest in Russian formalism or in the use of poetry to expand language's expressive possibilities, these are, of course, touchstones of O'Hara's verse.

Shapiro, furthermore, shares O'Hara's interest in narrative in his "I do this I do that" poems. Shapiro's use of what Fink calls with respect to *A Burning Interior* (2002) an "uncanny narrative," which, in turn, holds his poems together, maintains a place for an identifiable voice.[56] Shapiro recognizes that it is impossible to escape narrative, and, therefore, poetic voice, in lyrical poetry. In a 1990 interview with Joseph Lease, for example, he states, "I think if you're going to give up one form of storytelling you're going to have to do it another way."[57] Fisk correctly points out that Shapiro's stance for narrative is, perhaps, a more convincing treatment of the question of the relationship between voice and language than those that have followed Bernstein and Perelman.

In *January* (1965), for example, while Shapiro narrates recognizable events in the fist person, events that provide the context and the occasion for the expression of emotion or feeling in the poems, he uses the absurd and parataxis to prevent the meaning of the poem from being reduced to the meaning of the words themselves. "From Travel," for example, is a poem that is about the fear of oblivion and stasis, of losing one's location in time and space. However, rather than speaking to us, the "I" of the poem addresses the wind, following the example of O'Hara in "Les Etiquettes Jaunes" (1950) and "A True Account of Talking to the Sun at Fire Island" (1958) in which the poet in a sort of panic addresses the material world:

> Look, wind, I have run out of motion.
> The four animals who wanted me now refuse
> to have me; now that they have caught me,
> and I seemed so desirable when I was running away.
> The city limits are a kind of new dream for me.
> I used to think a few blocks meant the country.[58]

Again, following O'Hara, the paradox of desire for Shapiro is that it is characterized by a constant yearning to possess someone or something, a yearning that then disappears once the person or thing is possessed. In this case, however, the poet himself is the possessed, and the lack of desire for him he sees in others (now that he has been "caught" by them) precipitates a loss of sense of self. As the poem progresses, the paranoia of losing one's sense of self is expressed without the poem becoming a sort of confessional diatribe. The absurd element of the poet addressing the wind, the disconnected narrative, and the shifting voice of the poem work both to undermine our ability to reduce the poem to a mere confession and to express the slipping into oblivion itself. The short, direct, simple statements, furthermore, can be read with a certain amount of quickness. This expresses the poet's sense of franticness and is a means of preventing the slide into oblivion itself by keeping the poem "moving," so to speak. In this way, the poem embodies O'Hara's idea that art is a "barrier against death" (*EW*, 106). Though Shapiro, who wrote his doctoral dissertation on Ashbery at Columbia, is, throughout *January*, very much influenced by Ashbery's cool, meditative tone, he nevertheless mixes seemingly personal experiences with an "uncanny narrative" to create poems that have an effect similar to that of O'Hara's work. While Shapiro's later work has become less personal and less immediate, he continues to maintain a space for poetic voice in his work while, at the same time, retaining his formalist understanding of the end of poetry.

James Tate, too, follows O'Hara in a number of important respects. In his first volume of poetry, *The Lost Pilot* (1967), which won the Yale Series of Younger Poets Prize, Tate draws from the events of his life but presents them in a form that prevents us from reducing the words of the poem to a mere statement of confession. Using the absurd (which increases the gap between the "I" of the poet and the "I" of the poem in lyric poetry), Tate, like O'Hara, forces us to look at the words and form of the poem as the principal object of experience, while, at the same time, maintaining a tone and style that are personal and accessible. The events are recognizable, which helps to maintain the poem's relevance to the actual world. For example, in "Epithalamion for Tyler" (1968), a poem that could easily slide down the slippery slope of confessionalism, Tate keeps poetic image and form at the center of the poem through the absurd element of it:

> I thought I knew something
> about loneliness but
> you go to the stockyards
>
> buy a pig's ear and sew
> it on your couch. That, you
> said, is my best friend—we
>
> have spirited talks. Even
> then I thought: a man of
> such exquisite emptiness
>
> (and you cultivated it so)
> is ground for fine flowers.[59]

From the opening section, the poet both asserts and retracts the fact that he knows "something about loneliness." While the opening line implies that he does indeed know "something about loneliness," even if it is asserted in the negative form, this is compared to the unidentified interlocutor's "loneliness," which far surpasses that of the poet's loneliness and which is imaged by the pig's ear attached to the couch. The pathetic nature of this image at first underscores the depth of loneliness experienced by this unidentified interlocutor. However, the poet subtly undermines this image by implying that it is an exaggeration, "cultivated" by the interlocutor to look "exquisite." It is possible, furthermore, that the absurd image of the pig's ear attached to the couch could be a metaphor for confessional poems, which are the "fine flowers" of a "cultivated" emptiness—beautiful but superficial. If this is the case, it is ironic that Tate uses the image to avoid writing about his own loneliness—a loneliness that, if this reading of the poem is correct, is the more authentic.

While he does not note the influence of O'Hara, Brian Henry correctly notes that Tate's fascination with the absurd is, in part, a reaction against stasis and death.[60] According to Henry, Tate's use of monologues and sometimes surreal transitions "illuminates the flux of a person's thinking."[61] The goal, Henry argues, "is not a well-wrought urn but a constant movement within language."[62] This constant shifting of voice is one of the hallmarks of *The Lost Pilot*, according to Mark Ford, who argues that "goofy anecdotes, surreal lyrics, and metaphysical meditations are all characterized by a treacherous instability; at any moment the poem may succumb to the arbitrary dictates of some unfathomable syntax, and what appeared to be solid ground proves merely quicksand."[63] The results, according to Ford, are poems that are, on the one hand, grounded in the voice of the poet, and, on the other hand, strangely impersonal.[64]

In his work after *The Lost Pilot*, Tate continues to mix seemingly personal experiences with absurd images, a shifting voice, and parataxis. His tone, however, becomes both lighter and darker at the same time; through this the poet, following O'Hara, expresses a sort of humorous malaise. In "Poem (High in Hollywood Hills a door opens)" from *Oblivion Ha-Ha* (1970), for example, Tate writes, "O Desire! it is the beautiful dress // for which the proper occasion / never arises," and in "Crytozoa" from the same collection he writes, "I wish the stone lady would come home. / Parakeet or no parakeet / the night is a vial of lighterfluid."[65] Furthermore, in "Poem (I can't speak for the wind)" from *Viper Jazz* (1972), the poet compares himself to "a double-agent who tortures himself / and still will not speak."[66] In all of these examples, Tate mixes absurd images and literary references (such as the possible reference to *Wide Sargasso Sea* [1966] in "Crytozoa") with experiences from his personal life using parataxis and a shifting voice in an effort to use his life to create poems that, in O'Hara's words, are "all art" (*CP*, 499).

Thus, while Berrigan follows O'Hara in his understanding of artistic creation as a form of expression, and Bernstein and Silliman follow O'Hara in his "fronting" of poetic language, Shapiro and Tate draw from both of these aspects of O'Hara's work; and, in the end, it is this tension between poetry as a form of expression, coupled with elements of construction, and O'Hara's emphasis on the effects of the completed work that most distinguishes his poetics. O'Hara's work continues to influence new generations of poets. There are residues of O'Hara in the casual persona of Jon Anderson's *Death and Friends* (1970) and *In Sepia* (1974), the urban surrealism of Denis Johnson's *The Incognito Lounge* (1994), and the wry political commentary of Stephen Paul Miller's *Art Is Boring for the Same Reason We Stayed in Vietnam* (1992) and *Skinny Eighth Avenue* (2005), as well as the work of Mark Ford (b. 1962).

O'Hara's deep commitment to poetry itself allowed him to create a body of work that may indeed continue to influence poets for years to come. His hope that his work, like that of Gustave Courbet's, might bend "the ear of the outer world" has, in some respects, been fulfilled.

Notes

Introduction

1. Gilbert Sorrentino, "The New Note," in *Frank O'Hara: To Be True to a City*, ed. Scott Elledge (Ann Arbor: University of Michigan Press, 1990), 15.

2. Herbert Leibowitz, "A Pan Piping on the City Streets: *The Collected Poems of Frank O'Hara*," in *Frank O'Hara: To Be True to a City*, ed. Scott Elledge (Ann Arbor: University of Michigan Press, 1990), 24.

3. Thomas Byrom, review of *Frank O'Hara: Poet among Painters*, by Marjorie Perloff; *Early Writing*, by Frank O'Hara; and *Poems Retrieved*, by Frank O'Hara, *Times Literary Supplement*, January 27, 1978, 78.

4. Marjorie Perloff, "New Threshold, Old Anatomies: Contemporary Poetry and the Limits of Exegesis," *Iowa Review* 5, no. 1 (1974): 89.

5. David LeHardy Sweet, *Savage Sight / Constructed Noise: Poetic Adaptations of Painterly Techniques in the French and American Avant-Gardes* (Chapel Hill: University of North Carolina Press, 2003), 186.

6. To note but a few examples: Bruce Boone examines the notion of "textuality" in O'Hara's work based on "critical" definitions of that notion in the work of Roland Barthes, Jacques Derrida, and Frederic Jameson in a 1979 piece for the inaugural issue of *Social Text;* Mutlu Konuk Blasing relies heavily on Derrida's "La parole soufflée" in a 1982 article on O'Hara for *Contemporary Literature;* John Lowney uses Jameson's theories on "pastiche" in his 1991 essay on O'Hara in *Contemporary Literature;* and in *PMLA* Gregory W. Bredbeck couples O'Hara and Barthes in a 1993 essay on what he calls "homosexual semiotics." See Bruce Boone, "Gay Language as Political Praxis: The Poetry of Frank O'Hara," *Social Text* 1 (1979): 59–92; Mutlu Konuk Blasing, "Frank O'Hara's Poetics of Speech: The Example of 'Biotherm,'" *Contemporary Literature* 23, no. 1 (1982): 52–64; John Lowney, "The 'Post-Anti-Esthetic' Poetics of Frank O'Hara," *Contemporary Literature* 32, no. 2 (1991): 244–64; and Gregory W. Bredbeck, "B/O-Barthes's Text / O'Hara's Trick," *PMLA* 108, no. 2 (1993): 268–82. In addition to these articles there is the critical work of the "L=A=N=G=U=A=G=E" poets, in particular that of Charles Bernstein (b. 1940) and Bob Perelman (b. 1947), who treat the link between O'Hara's work and poststructuralism as a given. See Charles Bernstein, "Stray Straws, Straw Men," in *Content's Dream* (Los Angeles: Sun and Moon Press, 1986), 40–49; Bob Perelman, *The Marginalization of Poetry: Language Writing and Literary History* (Princeton, NJ: Princeton University Press, 1996). Despite this, and somewhat strangely, Lytle Shaw claims in his introductory chapter to *Frank O'Hara: The Poetics of Coterie* (2006) that the "interpretive language" that currently "constitutes the field" in O'Hara criticism is the application of O'Hara's own words in texts such as "Personism." See Lytle Shaw, *Frank O'Hara: The Poetics of Coterie* (Iowa City: University of Iowa Press, 2006), 10–11. The example

he cites to prove his point, however, is Bill Berkson and Joe LeSueur, eds., *Homage to Frank O'Hara*, (Bolinas, CA: Big Sky, 1978), 23839 n. 13. It is important to note that this volume, published over twenty years ago, was not edited by critics but by two of O'Hara's friends; and instead of critical appraisals of O'Hara's works, it contains a mix of poems, letters, memories, and reviews written by O'Hara's friends and acquaintances to *commemorate* O'Hara's death. Shaw is right, of course, that the book is both "rich and frustrating" (Shaw, *Frank O'Hara*, 11). However, it is hardly an example of the approach to O'Hara's work that has held court over the past twenty years.

7. Hazel Smith, *Hyperscapes in the Poetry of Frank O'Hara: Difference/Homosexuality/Topography* (Liverpool: Liverpool University Press, 2000), 9, 1.

8. Ibid., 11.

9. Ibid., 1.

10. André Breton, *Manifestoes of Surrealism*, trans. Richard Seaver and Helen R. Lane (Ann Arbor: University of Michigan Press, 1969), 26; Stéphane Mallarmé, "Crisis in Poetry," in *Mallarmé: Selected Prose Poems, Essays, and Letters*, ed., and trans. Bardford Cook (Baltimore: Johns Hopkins University Press, 1956), 38.

11. Guillaume Apollinaire, *The Cubist Painters*, trans. Peter Read (Berkeley and Los Angeles: University of California Press, 2002), 35–36.

12. Sweet, *Savage Sight*, 44–48.

13. Perloff runs into a similar problem in her use of "surface" and "indeterminacy" in *The Poetics of Indeterminacy: Rimbaud to Cage* (Princeton, NJ: Princeton University Press, 1980). As Paul Breslin notes in an insightful review of the book: "There is some sliding in Perloff's use of the word 'indeterminacy.' At times it refers to a severance of correspondences: instead of referring the surface of a text to a 'deeper' meaning behind it, as we do in interpreting a Symbolist poem, we must stop at the surface. This metaphor of surface and depth obscures the fact that there are more than two levels of correspondence in question: the correspondence of words to concepts, of concepts to states of affairs, and of states of affairs themselves to some implied spiritual state of which they are Eliotic 'objective correlatives.' . . . Such distinctions would have provided a way of explaining the obvious differences among Perloff's indeterminist writers, and they would have allowed a more rigorous definition of the senses in which a work can and cannot be 'indeterminate.'" Paul Breslin, review of *The Poetics of Indeterminacy: Rimbaud to Cage*, by Marjorie Perloff, *Modern Philology* 81, no. 3 (1984): 336.

14. Pepe Karmel, *Picasso and the Invention of Cubism* (New Haven, CT: Yale University Press, 2003), 14–15.

15. Hans Hofmann, *The Search for the Real and Other Essays*, ed. Sara T. Weeks and Bartlett H. Hayes Jr. (Cambridge, MA: MIT Press, 1967), 45.

16. Hans Hofmann, "The Color Problem in Pure Painting—Its Creative Origin," in *Hans Hofmann: A Retrospective*, ed. Karen Wilken (New York: George Braziller, 2003), 40–42.

17. Sweet, *Savage Sight*, 15.

18. For more on Salutati's definition of *poeticum narrationem*, see Alan Fisher, "Three Meditations on the Destruction of Vergil's Statue: The Early Humanist Theory of Poetry," *Renaissance Quarterly* 40, no. 4 (Winter 1987): 609–10; and Richard Waswo, "The 'Autonomy of Art' Is a Wish, Not a Fact," *Criticism* 22, no. 4 (Fall 1980): 350.

19. Robert Goodnough, "Pollock Paints a Picture," *ArtNews* 50, no. 3 (May 1951):

60; Harold Rosenberg, "The American Action Painters," *ArtNews* 51, no. 8 (December 1952): 22.

20. There have, of course, been a few studies that have compared O'Hara's work with the work of other poets. James E. B. Breslin examines O'Hara in the context of the "modern" lyric in his excellent *From Modern to Contemporary* (1983), and Geoff Ward treats O'Hara in the context of other New York poets such as Ashbery and Koch in *Statues of Liberty: The New York School of Poets* (London: Palgrave 1993). While these are very helpful studies of O'Hara's style, each devotes but one chapter to O'Hara. Other works that examine O'Hara's style with respect to other poets are histories, such as David Perkins' two-volume *A History of Modern Poetry* (Cambridge, MA: Harvard University Press 1976, 1987), the *Columbia Literary History of the United States* (New York: Columbia University Press, 1988), edited by Emory Elliot, and *The Cambridge History of American Literature* (Cambridge: Cambridge University Press, 1994–2004), edited by Sacvan Bercovitch. As helpful as the histories are, in the end they are too predetermined by the period terms "modern" and "postmodern," which juxtapose the "personal" and "spontaneous" writing style of so-called postmodern poets such as O'Hara against the "academic" writing style of so-called modern poets. How O'Hara might be unlike other "postmodern" poets and how he might be similar to "modern" ones is rarely explored in detail in such histories, because it is excluded a priori by the logic of the period term paradigm. For more on the problems of period terms with respect to O'Hara's work, see Micah Mattix, "Periodization and Difference," *New Literary History* 35, no. 4 (2004): 685–97. As Keith Waldrop eloquently puts it in *The Locality Principle* (Berkeley, CA: Avec Books, 1995), "The past lies in layers, not neatly in calendar years, but folded over sometimes like earth strata—uneven" (ibid., 66). To assume otherwise—to cut up the past into neat calendar years, or period terms—is to be blind to the inherent "messiness" of the past.

21. Charles Altieri, *Enlarging the Temple: New Directions in American Poetry during the 1960s* (Lewisburg, PA: Bucknell University Press, 1979), 78.

22. Ibid., 116.

1. "Memorial Day" 1950

1. Apollinaire, *Cubist Painters*, 38.

2. Ibid., 19.

3. Ibid.

4. Ibid., 20, 39–40.

5. Apollinaire writes, for example, that "Picasso studies an object like a surgeon dissecting a corpse" and that in order to re-create the human figure in his work, Picasso had to "assassinate himself as scientifically and methodically as a great surgeon" (ibid., 13, 38).

6. See, for example, Ronald Bush, "Art versus the Descent of the Iconoclasts: Cultural Memory in Ezra Pound's *Pisan Cantos*," in *American Poetry: Whitman to the Present*, ed. Robert Rehder and Patrick Vincent Swiss Papers in English Language and Literature (SPELL) 18, (Tübingen: Gunter Narr Verlag, 2006), 87–112.

7. Werner Spies, "An Open-Ended Oeuvre," in *Max Ernst: Dada and the Dawn of Surrealism*, trans. John Gabriel, ed. Simon Haviland (Munich: Prestel Verlag and the Menil Collection, 1993), 27.

8. Ibid.

9. Eberhard Fisch, *"Guernica" by Picasso: A Study of the Picture and Its Context*, trans. James Hotchkiss (Lewisburg, PA: Bucknell University Press, 1988), 22–23.

10. Pablo Picasso, *Picasso in His Words*, trans. and ed. Hiro Clark (San Francisco: Collins Publishers, 1993), 39.

11. Ibid.

12. Paul Klee, *Paul Klee on Modern Art*, trans. Paul Findlay, ed. Herbert Read (London: Faber and Faber, 1949), 51.

13. Paul Klee, *The Thinking Eye*, trans. Ralph Manheim, ed. Jürg Spiller (New York: George Wittenborn, 1961), 17.

14. Edward Brown tells the story of Mayakovsky's last public appearance, which was a poetry reading at the Plekhanov Auditorium of the Institute of the National Economy in Moscow. Following the reading of a poem that, given its paean to communism, should have caused little problem, Mayakovsky entered into a long debate with the audience with respect to the use of harsh language in poetry and obscure imagery, among other things. The night ended with students questioning Mayakovsky's communist commitments. He shot himself five days later. Edward J. Brown, *Mayakovsky: A Poet in the Revolution* (Princeton, NJ: Princeton University Press, 1973), 12–26.

15. Angela Livingstone, introduction to *Pasternak on Art and Creativity*, ed. Angela Livingstone (Cambridge: Cambridge University Press, 1985), 2.

16. Marina Tsvetaeva, "Art in the Light of Conscience," in *Modern Russian Poets on Poetry*, trans. Angela Livingstone and V. S. Coe, ed. Carl R. Proffer (Ann Arbor, MI: Ardis, 1976), 148.

17. Karmel, *Picasso*, 4.

18. Sweet, *Savage Sight*, 200.

19. For more on dolls in Rilke, see Eva-Maria Simms, "Uncanny Dolls: Images of Death in Rilke and Freud," *New Literary History* 27, no. 4 (Autumn 1996): 663–77.

20. Breton, *Manifestoes of Surrealism*, 14, 124.

21. Sweet, *Savage Sight*, 200. It is worth noting that O'Hara's corrective perhaps applies to more than just the surrealists. As Jeff Encke notes, the line, for example, also evokes the opening quote from Yeats's *Responsibilities* (1914), "In dreams begins responsibility," which Yeats attributes to an "old play," as well as Delmore Schwartz's book of short stories *In Dreams Begin Responsibilities*, published in 1938. Jeff Encke, "Why I Am Not a Manifestor: Postwar Avant-Gardism and the Manifestos of Frank O'Hara," *Octopus Magazine* 3 (2003)) http://www.octopusmagazine.com/ issue03/ encke_ohara.html; William Butler Yeats, *The Collected Poems of W. B. Yeats*, ed. Richard J. Finneran (New York: Scribner, 1996), 100; Delmore Schwartz, *In Dreams Begin Responsibilities and Other Stories* (New York: New Directions, 1978). James Logenbach remarks that the source of Yeats's quote is, in fact, Nietzsche. James Logenbach, *Stone Cottage: Pound, Yeats and Modernism* (Oxford: Oxford University Press, 1998), 159. Though Logenbach does not specify where in Nietzsche, it is likely that it is Nietzsche's remark on dreams in *The Dawn of Day* (1881), "You would wish to be responsible for everything except your dreams! What miserable weakness, what lack of logical courage! Nothing contains more of your own work than your dreams! Nothing belongs to you so much! Substance, form, duration, actor, spectator—in these comedies you act as your complete selves!" Frederick Nietzsche, *The Dawn of Day*, trans. J. M. Kennedy, vol. 9 of *The Complete Works of Frederick Nietzsche*, ed. Oscar Levy (New York: Russell and Russell, 1964), 131–32.

22. Livingstone, introduction, 3–4.

23. Boris Pasternak, *Safe Conduct: An Early Autobiography, and Other Works*, trans. Beatrice Scott (New York: New Directions, 1958), 30–31.

24. Eudo Mason, *Rilke* (London: Oliver and Boyd, 1963), 66.

25. Livingstone, introduction, 16.

26. William Carlos Williams, *The Collected Poems of William Carlos Williams*, ed. Christopher MacGowan (New York: New Directions, 1991), 2:54.

27. Apollinaire, *Cubist Painters*, 39.

28. That O'Hara disagreed with his real father regarding the extent to which we can make sense of death is clear in his poem "To My Dead Father" (1953) in which O'Hara asks his father not to insist "that I be other than your / strange son understanding / minor miracles not death" (*CP*, 161).

29. As an aside, this an important corrective to Lytle Shaw's claim that O'Hara is preoccupied in his poems with establishing an alternative "kinship structure." We find the poet here imaginatively reconciling himself to his father by becoming, in a common literary trope, the child-parent to his biological father (Shaw, *Frank O'Hara*, 6, 19).

30. In his *Digressions on Some Poems by Frank O'Hara*, Joe LeSueur, on more than one occasion, attributes to O'Hara an almost heroic confidence in his own greatness. Joseph LeSueur, *Digressions on Some Poems by Frank O'Hara: A Memoir* (New York: Farrar, Straus and Giroux, 2003), xxv. From his poems, however, we know that he often experienced his share of self-doubt. For example, in "At Joan's" (1959), O'Hara writes: "I sit at the marble top / sorting poems, miserable / the little lamp flows feebly / I don't glow at all." And in "Adieu to Norman, Bon Jour to Joan and Jean-Paul" (1959), he writes: "it is good to be several floors up in the dead of night / wondering whether you are any good or not / and the only decision you can make is that you did it" (*CP*, 327, 328).

31. Charles Olson, *Collected Prose*, ed. Donald Allen and Benjamin Friedlander (Berkeley and Los Angeles: University of California Press, 1997), 242.

32. Quoted in Mason, *Rilke*, 40; quoted in Livingstone, introduction, 12.

33. Frank O'Hara, "Paul Klee," *ArtNews* 53, no. 1 (March 1954): 41.

34. Karmel, *Picasso*, 8–9.

35. Frank O'Hara, "Cubism to 1918," *ArtNews* 52, no. 9 (January 1954): 65.

36, Frank O'Hara, "George Hartigan," *ArtNews* 52, no. 10 (February 1954): 45.

37. Frank O'Hara, "Three Sculptors," *ArtNews* 52, no. 8 (December 1953): 42.

38. Frank O'Hara, "Bennett Bradbury," *ArtNews* 52, no. 8 (December 1953): 65.

39. Frank O'Hara, "Miles Forst," *ArtNews* 53, no. 3 (May 1954): 43.

2. *Second Avenue*

1. Koch writes: "Frank and I both wrote long poems in 1953 (*Second Avenue* and *When the Sun Tries to Go On*). I had no clear intention of writing a 2400-line poem (which it turned out to be) before Frank said to me, on seeing the first 72 lines—which I regarded as a poem by itself—'Why don't you go on with it as long as you can?' Frank at this time decided to write a long poem too; I can't remember how much his decision to write such a poem had to do with his suggestion to me to write mine. While we were writing our long poems, we would read each other the results daily

over the telephone. This seemed to inspire us a good deal." Kenneth Koch, "A Note on Frank O'Hara in the Early Fifties," in *Homage to Frank O'Hara*, ed. Bill Berkson and Joe LeSueur (Bolinas, CA: Big Sky, 1978), 27.

2. John Ashbery claims, for example, that while *Second Avenue* is a useful experiment in attempting "to plot a not-yet-existent tradition with reference to what it was and what it wasn't," it is ultimately an unsatisfactory poem because of obfuscation (*CP*, ix). It "would not be necessary," Ashbery concludes, for O'Hara to make such an attempt again (*CP*, ix). Marjorie Perloff makes a similar, though more nuanced, remark when she writes that after *Second Avenue*, "O'Hara begins to put what we might call 'straight Surrealism' behind him" (*FOH*, 74). While she identifies a number of aspects of the poem that are clearly not surrealistic, Perloff, following Ashbery, nevertheless concludes that "[i]n the poems of 1954–1961, O'Hara's great period, we can no longer identify the echoes of Péret or Tzara or Desnos as readily; Surrealism has now been assimilated into an American idiom" (*FOH*, 74). O'Hara's "great period," as Perloff calls it, is the period in which he wrote the majority of what he calls his "I do this I do that" poems, in which he wrote in a direct and personal tone of the seeming insignificant details of a particular day.

3. Frank O'Hara to Barney Rosset, February 29, 1956.

4. Sweet, *Savage Sight*, 183.

5. For more on O'Hara's notion of free choice, see Michael Clune, "'Everything We Want': Frank O'Hara and the Aesthetics of Free Choice," *PMLA* 120, no. 1 (January 2005): 181–96.

6. Jeffrey Wechsler, *Surrealism and American Art, 1931–1947*, (New Brunswick, NJ: Rutgers University Art Gallery, 1976), 54–56.

7. Ibid., 63.

8. Robert Motherwell, "The Modern Painter's World," in *The Writings of Robert Motherwell*, ed. Dore Ashton (Berkeley and Los Angeles: University of California Press, 2007), 33.

9. Robert Hobbs, "Surrealism and Abstract Expressionism: From Psychic to Plastic Automatism," in *Surrealism USA*, ed. Isabelle Dervaux (New York: National Academy Museum, Hatje Cantz Publishers, 2005), 59–60.

10. Brad Gooch, *City Poet: The Life and Times of Frank O'Hara* (New York: Harper, 1994), 206.

11. John Milton, *The Complete Poems*, ed. John Leonard (New York: Penguin, 1998), 21.

12. Ibid.

13. Ibid.

14. Ibid.

15. Peter J. Sheehan, "Crane's 'Moment Fugue,'" *The Explicator* 31 (1978): 151.

16. Hart Crane, *Complete Poems and Selected Letters*, ed. Langdon Hammer (New York: Library of America, 2006), 87.

17. In *Song of Myself*, Whitman writes: "Do I contradict myself? / Very well then I contradict myself, / (I am large, I contain multitudes)." Walt Whitman, *Leaves of Grass*, ed. Sculley Bradley and Harold Blodgett (New York: New York University Press, 1965), lines 1324–26.

18. Mary McCarthy, "A Prince of Shreds and Patches," in *Focus on Shakespearean Films*, ed. Charles W. Eckert (New York: Prentice Hall, 1972), 66.

19. Gregory Machacek, "Allusion," *PMLA* 122, no. 2 (March 2007): 530.

3. Naming Things

1. Paul Goodman, "Advance-Guard Writing, 1900–1950," *Kenyon Review* 13, no. 3 (Summer 1951): 375–76.

2. Williams, *Collected Poems*, 2:202

3. Ibid., 1:203.

4. James E. B. Breslin, "Frank O'Hara," in *Frank O'Hara: To Be True to a City*, ed. Jim Elledge (Ann Arbor: University of Michigan Press, 1990), 261.

5. Peter Halter, *The Revolution in the Visual Arts and the Poetry of William Carlos Williams* (Cambridge: Cambridge University Press, 1994), 61.

6. Breslin, "Frank O'Hara," 262.

7. Ibid., 260.

8. Ibid., 262.

9. Ibid.

10. Hans-Georg Gadamer, *The Relevance of the Beautiful and Other Essays*, trans. Nicholas Walker, ed. Robert Bernasconi (Cambridge: Cambridge University Press, 1986), 44–45.

11. Ibid., 22–23.

12. Gooch, *City Poet*, 327.

13. Ibid.

14. Ibid., 328.

15. Goodman, "Advance-Guard Writing," 375.

4. "In Memory of My Feelings"

1. Mutlu Konuk Blasing, *The Art of Life: Studies in American Autobiographical Literature* (Austin: University of Texas Press, 1977), 147, 151.

2. Eric Mottram, "Frank O'Hara," in *American Poetry: The Modernist Ideal*, ed. Clive Bloom and Brian Docherty (New York: St. Martin's Press, 1995), 149–51.

3. Samuel Taylor Coleridge, *Biographia Literaria*, ed. James Engell and W. Jackson Bate (Princeton, NJ: Princeton University Press, 1983), 1:304.

4. While O'Hara's hiding behind a tree, rejecting his parental lineage, is evocative of D. W. Winnicott's later theories regarding the movement from nonself to self and the relationship between play and the self, his most well known works on the subject were first published after 1964. While Winnicott published a number of reviews and articles in specialized journals and his early *Critical Notes on Disorders of Childhood* in 1931, O'Hara is unlikely to have read any of these. For more on Winnicott, see Michael Jacobs, *D. W. Winnicott* (London: Sage, 1995), 146–47.

5. Frederick Nietzsche, *The Birth of Tragedy; or, Hellenism and Pessimism*, trans. William A. Haussman, vol. 1 of *The Complete Works of Frederick Nietzsche*, ed. Oscar Levy (New York: Russell and Russell, 1964), 27.

6. Christoph Cox, "Nietzsche, Dionysus, and the Ontology of Music," in *A Companion to Nietzsche*, ed. Keith Ansell Pearson (Oxford: Blackwell, 2006), 500.

7. Adrian Del Caro, "Nietzschean Self-Transformation and the Transformation of the Dionysian," in *Nietzsche, Philosophy and the Arts*, ed. Salim Kemal, Ivan Gaskell, and Daniel W. Conway (Cambridge: Cambridge University Press, 1998), 71.

8. Alfred North Whitehead, *Process and Reality* (New York: Free Press, 1957), 23.

9. Victor Lowe, *Understanding Whitehead* (Baltimore: Johns Hopkins University Press, 1962), 17.
10. Ibid.
11. Whitehead, *Process and Reality*, 28.
12. Ibid., 27.
13. Ibid., 26.
14. Rainer Maria Rilke, *Duino Elegies and The Sonnets to Orpheus*, trans. A. Poulin Jr. (Boston: Houghton Mifflin Company, 1977), 22.
15. Eugène Loudun, the pseudonym of Eugène Balleyquier, a frequent contributor of reviews to various art journals of the time, wrote this, for example, of Courbet's *L'atelier*: "What M. Courbet is looking for is the representation of people as they are, as ugly and as gross as he encounters them; in fact, the commoner they are the more he is attracted to the painting of them, it is one reason more; but everything is at the end of his brush, there is nothing generous, nothing lofty, nothing moral in the head which guides his hand; he invents nothing, has no imagination." Quoted in Bernard Goldman, "Realist Iconography: Intent and Criticism," *Journal of Aesthetics and Art Criticism* 18, no. 2 (1959): 186.
16. O'Hara wrote "In Memory of My Feelings" on what he thought was his thirtieth birthday. Twenty years after his death it was discovered that O'Hara was, in fact, born on March 27, 1926 rather than on June 27, the day which he had celebrated as his birthday his entire life. Russell Joseph O'Hara and Katherine Broderick, O'Hara's parents, married on September 14, 1925; then moved to Baltimore, where Katherine gave birth to O'Hara six months later, and only returned to Grafton after O'Hara was two years old (Gooch, *City Poet*, 14–15).
17. See *FOH*, 210 n. 7.
18. Martin Heidegger, *Being and Time*, trans. Joan Stambaugh (Albany: State University Press of New York Press, 1996), 120.
19. Gooch, *City Poet*, 283.

5. Love

1. Gooch, *City Poet*, 273.
2. Pasternak, *Safe Conduct*, 31.
3. John Donne, *The Complete Poetry and Prose of John Donne*, ed. Charles M. Coffic (New York: Modern Library, 1952), 421; Rainer Maria Rilke, *Letters to a Young Poet*, trans. M. D. Herter Norton (New York: W. W. Norton, 1934), 34.
4. Alan Feldman, *Frank O'Hara* (Boston: Twayne, 1979), 105.
5. Alfred, Lord Tennyson, *In Memoriam*, ed. Susan Shatto and Marion Shaw (Oxford: Clarendon Press, 1982), 59.

Conclusion: After O'Hara

1. Willis Barnstone, introduction to *Border of a Dream: Selected Poems of Antonio Machado*, trans. Willis Barnstone (Port Townsend, WA: Copper Canyon Press, 2003), xlix–liii.

2. Norma Louise Hutman, *Machado: A Dialogue with Time; Nature as an Expression of Temporality in the Poetry of Antonio Machado* (Albuquerque: University of New Mexico Press, 1969), 39–41.

3. Antonio Machado, *The Selected Poems of Antonio Machado*, trans. Betty Jean Craige (Baton Rouge: Louisiana State University Press, 1978), xv.

4. Jean Moréas, "Le symbolisme," *Figaro*, September 18, 1898, 150.

5. Ibid., 151.

6. See John Butler Davis, *Jean Moréas: A Critique of His Poetry and Philosophy* (The Hague: Mouton, 1967).

7. Hutman, *Machado*, 41.

8. Allen Ginsberg, forward to *Out of this World: An Anthology of the St. Mark's Poetry Project, 1966–1991*, ed. Anne Waldman (New York: Crown Publishers, 1991), xxiv.

9. Anne Waldman, introduction to *Out of This World: An Anthology of the St. Mark's Poetry Project, 1966–1991*, ed. Anne Waldman (New York: Crown Publishers, 1991), 3.

10. Ginsberg, forward, xxv–xxvi.

11. Waldman, introduction to *Out of This World*, 4.

12. Anne Waldman, introduction to *Nice to See You: Homage to Ted Berrigan*, ed. Anne Waldman (Minneapolis: Coffee House Press, 1991), vi–vii.

13. Waldman, historical notes in *Out of this World: An Anthology of the St. Mark's Poetry Project, 1966–1991*, ed. Anne Waldman (New York: Crown Publishers, 1991), 668–69.

14. Anne Waldman, *Fast Speaking Woman: Chants and Essays* (San Francisco: City Lights Books, 1975), 145.

15. Ron Padgett, "On *The Sonnets*," in *Nice to See You: Homage to Ted Berrigan*, ed. Anne Waldman (Minneapolis: Coffee House Press, 1991), 10.

16. Libbie Rifkin, "'Worrying about Making It': Ted Berrigan's Social Poetics," *Contemporary Literature* 38, no. 4 (2008): 641.

17. Ron Padgett, "Four French Poets and the Cubist Painters," in *The Straight Line: Writings on Poetry and Poets* (Ann Arbor: University of Michigan Press, 2000), 33.

18. Ibid., 33–34.

19. Ron Padgett, *Great Balls of Fire* (Minneapolis: Coffee House Press, 1990), 12.

20. Ibid.

21. Ibid., 12–13.

22. Ibid., 13.

23. Ibid., 14.

24. Ibid.

25. Padgett, "Four French Poets and the Cubist Painters," 34.

26. Clark Coolidge, "FO'H Notes," in *Homage to Frank O'Hara*, ed. Bill Berkson and Joe LeSueur (Bolinas, CA: Big Sky, 1988), 183.

27. Ibid.

28. Ibid.

29. Ibid.

30. Ibid., 185.

31. In her 1997 introduction to her reissued *Frank O'Hara*, Perloff herself notes Coolidge's response to O'Hara in "FO'H Notes" and sanctions his reading. She

writes that "perhaps it took a New York Poet *manqué* like Coolidge to understand that O'Hara's 'discreet'/'discrete' language (as opposed to the O'Hara mystique), far from sanctifying the 'natural,' the casual, and the unique speaking voice, was actually providing a groundwork for the new materialist poetics" (*FOH*, xxiv–xxv).

32. Charles Bernstein, "Stray Straw and Straw Men," in *Content's Dream* (Los Angeles: Sun and Moon Press, 1986), 41.

33. Ibid., 41, 44.

34. Charles Bernstein, "Three or Four Things I Know about Him," in *Content's Dream* (Los Angeles: Sun and Moon Press, 1986), 26.

35. Ibid.

36. Ibid.

37. Ibid., 27–28.

38. Ibid., 28–29.

39. Bernstein, "Stray Straws and Straw Men," 45–46.

40. Ibid., 41.

41. Ibid., 43.

42. Ron Silliman, "Who Speaks: Ventriloquism and the Self in the Poetry Reading," in *Close Listening: Poetry and the Performed Word*, ed. Charles Bernstein (Oxford: Oxford University Press, 1988), 362.

43. Perelman, *Marginalization of Poetry;* 158.

44. Ibid., 159.

45. In his interview with Edward Lucie-Smith, O'Hara criticizes Olson for his preoccupation with what O'Hara calls the "important utterance" (*SS*, 22).

46. Perelman, *Marginalization*, 159, 161.

47. Ibid., 164.

48. Kenneth Koch, "All the Imagination Can Hold (*The Collected Poems of Frank O'Hara*)," in *Homage to Frank O'Hara*, ed. Bill Berkson and Joe LeSueur (Bolinas, CA: Big Sky, 1978), 205.

49. Ibid.

50. Ibid., 206.

51. Bill Berkson, "Frank O'Hara and His Poems," in *Homage to Frank O'Hara*, ed. Bill Berkson and Joe LeSueur (Bolinas, CA: Big Sky, 1978), 163.

52. Kenneth Koch, "A Note on Frank O'Hara in the Early Fifties," in *Homage to Frank O'Hara*, ed. Bill Berkson and Joe LeSueur (Bolinas, CA: Big Sky, 1978), 27.

53. Ibid. It sometimes seems that Bernstein's and Perelman's rejection of poetic voice in O'Hara's poems is grounded in the very terms they claim to reject. Coolidge notes, for example, that O'Hara's work can sometimes be "embarrassing." And both Bernstein and Perelman reject O'Hara's "voice" because of its *lack of faithfulness* to certain materialistic presuppositions regarding what is and what is not real. These criticisms, in other words, are grounded in a predetermined notion of what counts as an authentic utterance and what does not. In the work of Bernstein and Perelman (both of whom use the term "critical" to mean "authentic"), for example, authentic utterances are defined as those utterances that foreground the material nature of language (though how much is unclear). Those that do not are inauthentic.

54. Thomas Fink, *The Poetry of David Shapiro* (Madison, NJ: Fairleigh Dickinson University Press, 1993), 15.

55. Ibid., 23.

56. Thomas Fink, "Uncanny Narrative in Shapiro's *A Burning Interior*," in *Burning*

Interiors: David Shapiro's Poetry and Poetics, ed. Thomas Fink and Joseph Lease (Madison, NJ: Fairleigh Dickinson University Press, 2007), 123–24.

57. Quoted in Fink, "Uncanny Narrative," 124.

58. David Shapiro, *New and Selected Poems* (1965–2006) (New York: Overlook Press, 2007), 14.

59. James Tate, *The Lost Pilot* (New Haven, CT: Yale University Press, 1967), 7.

60. Brian Henry, "Emersonian Transition in James Tate's *The Lost Pilot*," in *On James Tate*, ed. Brian Henry (Ann Arbor: University of Michigan Press, 2004), 85–86.

61. Ibid., 87.

62. Ibid.

63. Mark Ford, "Distance from Loved Ones," in *On James Tate*, ed. Brian Henry (Ann Arbor: University of Michigan Press, 2004), 107.

64. Ibid., 113.

65. James Tate, *Oblivion Ha-Ha* (Boston: Little, Brown and Co., 1970), 3, 9.

66. James Tate, *Viper Jazz* (Middletown, CT: Wesleyan University Press, 1972), 11.

Bibliography

Works by Frank O'Hara

O'Hara, Frank. *Art Chronicles, 1954–1966.* New York: George Braziller, 1975.

———. "Bennett Bradbury." *ArtNews* 52, no. 8 (December 1953): 65.

———. *The Collected Poems of Frank O'Hara.* Ed. Donald Allen. Berkeley and Los Angeles: University of California Press, 1995.

———. "Cubism to 1918." *ArtNews* 52, no. 9 (January 1954): 65.

———. *Early Writing.* Ed. Donald Allen. Bolinas, CA: Grey Fox, 1977.

———. "George Hartigan." *ArtNews* 52, no. 10 (February 1954): 45.

———. *Jackson Pollock.* New York: George Braziller, 1959.

———. *Love Poems (Tentative Title).* New York: Tibor de Nagy, 1965.

———. *Lunch Poems.* San Francisco: City Lights, 1964.

———. *Meditations in an Emergency.* New York: Grove Press, 1967.

———. "Miles Forst." *ArtNews* 53, no. 3 (May 1954): 43.

———. "Paul Klee." *ArtNews* 53, no. 1 (March 1954): 41.

———. *Poems Retrieved.* Ed. Donald Allen. San Francisco: Grey Fox, 2001.

———. *Robert Motherwell.* Garden City, NY: Doubleday, 1965.

———. *Second Avenue.* New York: Totem Press, 1960.

———. *Standing Still and Walking in New York.* Ed. Donald Allen. San Francisco: Grey Fox, 1975.

———. "Three Sculptors." *ArtNews* 52, no. 8 (December 1953): 42.

Unpublished Letters and Manuscripts of Frank O'Hara

Allen Collection of Frank O'Hara Letters. Archives and Special Collections at the Thomas J. Dodd Research Center, University of Connecticut Libraries.

Works by Others

Abrams, M. H. *The Mirror and the Lamp: Romantic Theory and the Critical Tradition.* Oxford: Oxford University Press, 1953.

Adamowicz, Elza. *Surrealist Collage in Text and Image: Dissecting the Exquisite Corpse.* Cambridge: Cambridge University Press, 1998.

Allen, Gay Wilson. "Walt Whitman: 'Cosmos-Inspired.'" In *Leaves of Grass: A Norton Critical Edition*, ed. Sculley Bradley and Harold W. Blodgett, 895–902. New York: W.W. Norton, 1973.

Altieri, Charles. "Contingency as Compositional Principle in Fifties Poetics." In *The Scene of My Selves: New York on New York School Poets*, ed. Terence Diggory and Stephen Paul Miller, 359–84. Orono, ME: National Poetry Foundation, 2001.

———. *Enlarging the Temple: New Directions in American Poetry during the 1960s*. Lewisburg, PA: Bucknell University Press, 1979.

———. "The Objectivist Tradition." In *The Objectivist Nexus: Essays in Cultural Poetics*, ed. Rachel Blau DuPlessis and Peter Quartermain, 25–36. Tuscaloosa: University of Alabama Press, 1999.

———. *Painterly Abstraction in Modernist American Poetry: The Contemporaneity of Modernism*. London: Cambridge University Press, 1989.

——— *Self and Sensibility in Contemporary American Poetry*. London: Cambridge University Press, 1984.

———. "The Significance of Frank O'Hara." *Iowa Review* 4, no. 3 (1973): 90–104.

Apollinaire, Guillaume. *Alcools*. Trans. Anne Hyde Greet. Berkeley: University of California Press, 1965.

———. *Calligrammes: Poems of Peace and War (1913–1916)*. Trans. Anne Hyde Greet. Berkeley: University of California Press, 1980.

———. *The Cubist Painters*. Trans. Peter Read. Berkeley: University of California Press, 2002.

———. "The New Spirit and the Poets." Trans. Roger Shattuck. In *Selected Writings*, 227–37. New York: New Directions, 1950.

Arnheim, Rudolf. "Accident and the Necessity of Art." In *Toward a Psychology of Art: Collected Essays*, 162–80. Berkeley: University of California Press, 1972.

———. "Emotion and Feeling in Psychology and Art." In *Toward a Psychology of Art: Collected Essays*, 303–19. Berkeley: University of California Press, 1972.

———. *Entropy and Art: An Essay on Disorder and Order*. Berkeley: University of California Press, 1971.

Ashbery, John. "Frank O'Hara's Question." *Book Week*, September 25, 1966, 6.

———. *Other Traditions*. Cambridge, MA: Harvard University Press, 2000.

———. *Selected Poems*. London: Carcanet Press, 1986.

———. *Self-Portrait in a Convex Mirror*. New York: Penguin, 1976.

———. *Three Poems*. New York: Viking, 1970.

Barfield, Owen. *History in English Words*. London: Faber and Faber, 1953.

Barnstone, Willis. Introduction to *Border of a Dream:Selected Poems of Antonio Machado*, trans. and ed. Willis Barnstone, i–liii. Port Townsend, WA: Copper Canyon Press, 2003.

Barthes, Roland, "The Death of the Author." Trans. Samuel Heath. In *Modern Literary Theory*, ed. Philip Rice and Patricia Waugh, 118–22. London: Arnold, 1996.

———. *The Pleasure of the Text*. Trans. Richard Miller. New York: Hill and Wang, 1975.

Bartlett, Lee. "What Is Language Poetry?" *Critical Inquiry* 12, no. 4 (1986): 741–52.

Baudelaire, Charles. *Les fleurs du mal.* Paris: Presses Pocket, 1981.

Beach, Christopher. *The Cambridge Introduction to Twentieth-Century American Poetry.* Cambridge: Cambridge University Press, 2003.

Beranger, Pierre Jean de. *Beranger's Poems.* Ed. William S. Walsh. Philadelphia: J. B. Lippincott Company, 1889.

Bercovitch, Sacvan, ed. *The Cambridge History of American Literature.* 8 vols. Cambridge: Cambridge University Press, 1994–2004.

———. *The Puritan Origins of the American Self.* New Haven, CT: Yale University Press, 1975.

Berkson, Bill. "Frank O'Hara and His Poems." In *Homage to Frank O'Hara*, ed. Bill Berkson and Joe LeSueur, 161–65. Bolinas, CA: Big Sky, 1978.

———. "Working with Joe." *Jacket Magazine* 16 (2002). http://jacketmagazine.com/16/br-berk.html.

Bernstein, Charles. "Stray Straws, Straw Men." In *Content's Dream*, 40–49. Los Angeles: Sun and Moon Press, 1986.

———. "Three or Four Things I Know about Him." In *Content's Dream*, 13–33. Los Angeles: Sun and Moon Press, 1986.

Bewell, Alan. *Wordsworth and the Enlightenment: Nature, Man and Society in the Experimental Poetry.* New Haven, CT: Yale University Press, 1989.

Blackmur, R. P. *Language as Gesture: Essays in Poetry.* London: George Allen and Unwin, 1954.

Blasing, Mutlu Konuk. *American Poetry: The Rhetoric of Its Forms.* New Haven, CT: Yale University Press, 1987.

———. *The Art of Life: Studies in American Autobiographical Literature.* Austin: University of Texas Press, 1977.

———. "Frank O'Hara's Poetics of Speech: The Example of 'Biotherm.'" *Contemporary Literature* 23, no. 1 (1982): 52–64.

———. *Politics and Form in Postmodern Poetry: O'Hara, Bishop, Ashbery, and Merrill.* London: Cambridge University Press, 1995.

Boone, Bruce. "Gay Language as Political Praxis: The Poetry of Frank O'Hara." *Social Text* 1 (Winter 1979): 59–92.

Bornstein, George. *The Postromantic Consciousness of Ezra Pound.* Victoria, BC: University of Victoria Press, 1977.

Bradley, A. C. "Poetry for Poetry's Sake." In *Oxford Lectures on Poetry*, 3–36. London: Macmillan, 1959.

Bredbeck, Gregory W. "B/O Barthes's Text / O'Hara's Trick." *PMLA* 108, no. 2 (1993): 268–82.

Breslin, James E. B. "Frank O'Hara." In *Frank O'Hara: To Be True to a City*, ed. Jim Elledge, 260–62. Ann Arbor: University of Michigan Press, 1990.

———. *From Modern to Contemporary: American Poetry, 1945–1965.* Chicago: University of Chicago Press, 1984.

———. "Poetry." In *Columbia Literary History of the United States*, ed. Emory Elliot et al., 1082–83. New York: Columbia University Press, 1988.

Breslin, Paul. Review of *The Poetics of Indeterminacy: Rimbaud to Cage*, by Marjorie Perloff. *Modern Philology* 81, no. 3 (February 1984): 333–36.

Breton, André. *Manifestes du surréalisme.* Paris: Gallimard, 1985.

———. *Manifestoes of Surrealism.* Trans. Richard Seaver and Helen R. Lane. Ann Arbor: University of Michigan Press, 1969.

———. *Le surréalisme et la peinture.* Paris: Gallimard, 1965.

Broad, C. D. *Kant: An Introduction.* Cambridge: Cambridge University Press, 1978.

Brossard, Olivier. "The Last Clean Shirt: A Film by Alfred Leslie and Frank O'Hara." *Jacket Magazine* 23 (2003). http://www.jacketmagazine.com/23/bross-ohara.html.

Brown, Edward J. *Mayakovsky: A Poet in the Revolution.* Princeton, NJ: Princeton University Press, 1973.

Bush, Ronald. "Art versus the Descent of the Iconoclasts: Cultural Memory in Ezra Pound's *Pisan Cantos.*" In *Swiss Papers in English Language and Literature (SPELL) 18: American Poetry from Whitman to the Present,* ed. Robert Rehder and Patrick Vincent, 87–112. Tübingen: Gunter Narr Verlag, 2006.

Byrom, Thomas. Review of *Frank O'Hara: Poet among Painters,* by Marjorie Perloff; *Early Writing* by Frank O'Hara; and *Poems Retrieved,* by Frank O'Hara. *Times Literary Supplement,* January 27, 1978, 78.

Cambfield, William A. *Max Ernst: Dada and the Dawn of Surrealism.* Munich: Prestel Verlag and the Menil Collection, 1993.

Carrol, Paul. "An Impure Poem about July 17, 1959." In *The Poem in Its Skin,* 60–69. London: Big Table, 1968.

Cavalcanti, Guido. *The Complete Poems.* Trans. Marc A. Cirigliano. New York: Ithaca Press, 1992.

Caws, Mary Ann. *The Poetry of Dada and Surrealism.* Princeton, NJ: Princeton University Press, 1970.

Chénieux-Gendron, Jacqueline. *Le surréalisme.* Paris: Presses Universitaires de France, 1984.

Clune, Michael. "'Everything We Want': Frank O'Hara and the Aesthetics of Free Choice." *PMLA* 120, no. 1 (January 2005): 181–96

Coleridge, Samuel Taylor. *Biographia Literaria.* Ed. James Engell and Jackson Bate. 2 vols. In *The Collected Works of Samuel Taylor Coleridge,* ed. Kathleen Coburn. Princeton, NJ: Princeton University Press, 1983.

Coolidge, Clark. "FO'H Notes." In *Homage to Frank O'Hara,* ed. Bill Berkson and Joe LeSueur, 183–85. Bolinas, CA: Big Sky, 1978.

Cox, Christoph. "Nietzsche, Dionysus, and the Ontology of Music." In *A Companion to Nietzsche,* ed. Keith Ansell Pearson, 495–513.Oxford: Blackwell, 2006.

Crain, Caleb. "Frank O'Hara's 'Fired' Self.'" *American Literary History* 9, no. 2 (1997): 287–308.

Crane, Hart. *Complete Poems and Selected Letters.* Ed. Langdon Hammer. New York: Library of America, 2006.

Croce, Benedetto. *Aesthetic as Science of Expression and General Linguistic.* Trans. Douglas Ainsli. London: Vision Press, 1953.

Daix, Pierre. *Picasso.* New York: Praeger, 1965.

Damon, Maria. "Queer Cities." In *A Concise Companion to Twentieth-Century American Poetry,* ed. Stephen Fredman, 95–112. London: Blackwell, 2005.

Davis, John Butler. *Jean Moréas: A Critique of His Poetry and Philosophy*. The Hague: Mouton, 1967.

Del Caro, Adrian. "Nietzschean Self-Transformations and the Transformation of the Dionysian." In *Nietzsche, Philosophy and the Arts*, ed. Salim Kemal, Ivan Gaskell, and Daniel W. Conway, 70–91. Cambridge: Cambridge University Press, 1988.

Descartes, René. *Discours de la méthode / Discourse on the Method*. Trans., and ed. George Heffernan. Notre Dame, IN: University of Notre Dame Press, 1994.

Diggory, Terence. "Community Intimate or Inoperative: New York School of Poets and Politics from Paul Goodman to Jean-Luc Nancy." In *The Scene of My Selves: New York on New York School Poets*, ed. Terence Diggory and Stephen Paul Miller, 13–32. Orono, ME: National Poetry Foundation, 2001.

Donne, John. *The Complete Poetry and Prose of John Donne*. Ed. Charles M. Coffic. New York: Modern Library, 1952.

Donnelley, Strachan. "The Philosopher's Poet: Boris Pasternak, *Dr. Zhivago*, and Whitehead's Cosmological Vision." *Process Studies* 13, no. 1 (Spring 1983): 45–58.

Dostal, Robert J. "Time and Phenomenology in Husserl and Heidegger." In *The Cambridge Companion to Heidegger*, Charles B. Guignon, 120–148. 2nd ed. Cambridge: Cambridge University Press, 2006.

Durrant, Geoffrey. *Wordsworth and the Great System: A Study of Wordsworth's Poetic Universe*. Cambridge: Cambridge University Press, 1970.

Eliot, T. S. *The Complete Poems and Plays*. London: Faber and Faber, 1969.

———. *The Selected Prose of T. S. Eliot*. Ed. Frank Kermode. London: Faber and Faber, 1975.

Elliot, Emory, ed. *Columbia Literary History of the United States*. New York: Columbia University Press, 1988.

Ellmann, Maud. *The Poetics of Impersonality: T. S. Eliot and Ezra Pound*. Brighton, England: Harvester Press, 1987.

Encke, Jeff. "Why I Am Not a Manifestor: Postwar Avant-Gardism and the Manifestos of Frank O'Hara." *Octopus Magazine* 3 (2003). http://www. octopusmagazine.com/issue03/encke_ohara.html.

Ernst, Max. *Beyond Painting and Other Writings by the Artist and His Friends*. Trans. Ralph Manheim and Dorothea Tanning. Ed. Robert Motherwell. New York: Wittenborn, Shultz, 1948.

Feldman, Alan. *Frank O'Hara*. Boston: Twayne, 1979.

Ferguson, Russell. *In Memory of My Feelings: Frank O'Hara and American Art*. Berkeley and Los Angeles: University of California Press, 1999.

Fink, Thomas. *The Poetry of David Shapiro*. Madison, NJ: Fairleigh Dickinson University Press, 1993.

———. "Uncanny Narrative in Shapiro's *A Burning Interior*." In *Burning Interiors: David Shapiro's Poetry and Poetics*, ed. Thomas Fink and Joseph Lease, 120–36. Madison, NJ: Fairleigh Dickinson University Press, 2007.

Fisch, Eberhard. *"Guernica" by Picasso: A Study of the Picture and Its Context*. Trans. James Hotchkiss. 2nd ed. Lewisburg, PA: Bucknell University Press, 1988.

Fisher, Alan. "Three Meditations on the Destruction of Vergil's Statue: The Early

Humanist Theory of Poetry." *Renaissance Quarterly* 40, no. 4 (Winter 1987): 607–35.

Forbes, Deborah. *Sincerity's Shadow: Self-Consciousness in British Romantic and Mid-Twentieth-Century American Poetry.* Cambridge, MA: Harvard University Press, 2004.

Ford, Mark. "Distance from Loved Ones." In *On James Tate*, ed. Brian Henry, 107–14. Ann Arbor: University of Michigan Press, 2004.

Frede, Dorothea. "The Question of Being: Heidegger's Project." In *The Cambridge Companion to Heidegger*, ed. Charles B. Guignon, 42–69. 2nd ed. Cambridge: Cambridge University Press, 2006.

Fredman, Stephen. "Mysticism: Neo-paganism, Buddhism, and Christianity." In *A Concise Companion to Twentieth-Century American Poetry*, ed. Stephen Fredman, 191–211. Oxford: Blackwell, 2005.

———. *Poet's Prose: The Crisis in American Verse.* Cambridge: Cambridge University Press, 1983.

Fried, Michael. *Courbet's Realism.* Chicago: University of Chicago Press, 1990.

Gadamer, Hans-Georg. *The Relevance of the Beautiful and Other Essays.* Trans. Nicholas Walker. Ed. Robert Bernasconi. Cambridge: Cambridge University Press, 1986.

Gemünden, Gerd. "The Depth of the Surface; or, What Rolf Dieter Brinkmann Learned from Andy Warhol." *German Quarterly* 68, no. 3 (1995): 235–50.

Genet, Jean. *Our Lady of the Flowers.* Trans. Bernard Frechtman. New York: Modern Library, 1965.

Gide, André. *The Counterfeiters.* Trans. Dorothy Bussy. New York: The Modern Library, 1955.

———. "Dada." Trans. Justin O'Brian. In *Pretexts: Reflections on Literature and Morality*, ed. Justin O'Brian, 289–93. New York: Meridian Books, 1959.

———. "The Limits of Art." Trans. Jeffrey C. Carre. In *Pretexts: Reflections on Literature and Morality*, ed. Justin O'Brian, 40–48. New York: Meridian Books, 1959.

Ginsberg, Allen. *Collected Poems, 1947–1980.* London: Penguin, 1987.

———. Foreword to *Out of This World: An Anthology of the St. Mark's Poetry Project, 1966–1991*, ed. Anne Waldman, xxiv–xxx. New York: Crown Publishers, 1991.

Glavey, Brian. "Frank O'Hara Nude with Boots: Queer *Ekphrasis* and the Statuesque Poet." *American Literature* 79, no. 4 (December 2007): 781–806.

Goble, Mark. "'Our Country's Black and White Past': Film and the Figures of History in Frank O'Hara." *American Literature* 71, no. 1 (1999): 57–92.

Goldman, Bernard. "Realist Iconography: Intent and Criticism." *Journal of Aesthetics and Art Criticism* 18, no. 2 (1959): 183–92.

Gooch, Brad. *City Poet: The Life and Times of Frank O'Hara.* New York: Knopf, 1993.

Goodman, Paul. "Advance-Guard Writing, 1900–1950." *Kenyon Review* 13, no. 3 (Summer 1951): 357–80.

Goodnough, Robert. "Pollock Paints a Picture." *ArtNews* 50, no. 3 (May 1951): 38–41, 60–61.

Graham, Gordon. *Philosophy of the Arts: An Introduction to Aesthetics.* London: Routledge, 2005.

Guignon, Charles B. Introduction to *The Cambridge Companion to Heidegger*, ed. Charles B. Guignon, 2nd ed. 1–41. Cambridge: Cambridge University Press, 2006.

Hallberg, Robert von. "Avant-Gardes." In vol. 8 of *The Cambridge History of American Literature*, ed. Sacvan Bercovitch, 83–122. Cambridge: Cambridge University Press, 1996.

Halter, Peter. *The Revolution in the Visual Arts and the Poetry of William Carlos Williams*. Cambridge: Cambridge University Press, 1994.

Hamilton, Paul. *Coleridge's Poetics*. Oxford: Blackwell, 1983.

———. *Wordsworth*. Brighton, England: Harvester Press, 1986.

Haskins, Casey. "Kant, Autonomy, and Art for Art's Sake." *Journal of Aesthetics and Art Criticism* 48, no. 3 (1990): 235–37.

———. "Kant and the Autonomy of Art." *Journal of Aesthetics and Art Criticism* 47, no. 1 (1989): 43–54.

Heidegger, Martin. *Being and Time*. Trans. Joan Stambaugh. Albany: State University of New York Press, 1996.

Hellerstein, Marjorie. *Inventing the Real World: The Art of Alain Robbe-Grillet*. Selinsgrove, PA: Susquehanna University Press, 1998.

Henry, Brian. "Emersonian Transition in James Tate's *The Lost Pilot*." In *On James Tate*, ed. Brian Henry, 85–94. Ann Arbor: University of Michigan Press, 2004.

Herd, David. *John Ashbery and American Poetry*. London: Palgrave, 2000.

———. "Pleasure at Home: How Twentieth-Century American Poets Read the British." In *A Concise Companion to Twentieth-Century American Poetry*, ed. Stephen Fredman, 33–54. London: Blackwell, 2005.

Hobbs, Robert. "Surrealism and Abstract Expressionism: From Psychic to Plastic Automatism." In *Surrealism USA*, ed. Isabelle Dervaux, 56–65. New York: National Academy Museum and Hatje Cantz Publishers, 2005.

Hoffman, Katherine. "Elsa Dorfman: Portraits of Our Time." *Woman's Art Journal* 20, no. 2 (1999–2000): 24–28.

Hofmann, Hans. "The Color Problem in Pure Painting—Its Creative Origin." In *Hans Hofmann: A Retrospective*, ed. Karen Wilken, 39–43. New York: George Braziller, 2003.

———. *The Search for the Real and Other Essays*. Ed. Sara T. Weeks and Bartlett H. Hayes Jr. Cambridge, MA: MIT Press, 1967.

Hutman, Norma Louise. *Machado: A Dialogue with Time; Nature as an Expression of Temporality in the Poetry of Antonio Machado*. Albuquerque: University of New Mexico Press, 1969.

Jacobs, Michael. *D. W. Winnicott*. London: Sage, 1995.

Kagan, Andrew. *Paul Klee: Art and Music*. Ithaca, NY: Cornell University Press, 1983.

Kant, Immanuel. *Critique of Pure Reason*. Ed. and Trans. Paul Guyer and Allen Wood. Cambridge: Cambridge University Press, 1998.

Karmel, Pepe. *Picasso and the Invention of Cubism*. New Haven, CT: Yale University Press, 2003.

Keats, John. *The Poetical Works of John Keats*. Ed. H. W. Garrod. London: Oxford University Press, 1959.

———. *Selected Letters of John Keats*. Ed. Grant F. Scott. Rev. ed. Cambridge, MA: Harvard University Press, 2002.

Kermode, Frank. *Pleasure and Change: The Aesthetics of Canon*. Oxford: Oxford University Press, 2004.

Klee, Paul. *Paul Klee on Modern Art*. Trans. Paul Findlay, London: Faber and Faber, 1949.

———. *The Thinking Eye*. Trans. Ralph Manheim. Ed. Jürg Spiller. New York: George Wittenborn, 1961.

Koch, Kenneth. "All the Imagination Can Hold (*The Collected Poems of Frank O'Hara*)." In *Homage to Frank O'Hara*, ed. Bill Berkson and Joe LeSueur, 205–8. Bolinas, CA: Big Sky, 1978.

———. *The Art of Poetry: Poems, Parodies, Interviews, Essays, and Other Work*. Ann Arbor: University of Michigan Press, 1996.

———. "A Note on Frank O'Hara in the Early Fifties." In *Homage to Frank O'Hara*, ed. Bill Berkson and Joe LeSueur, 26–27. Bolinas, CA: Big Sky, 1978.

Leader, Zachery. "Wordsworth, Revision, and Personal Identity." *ELH* 63, no. 3 (1993): 651–83.

Legge, Elizabeth M. *Max Ernst: The Psychoanalytic Sources*. Ann Arbor: UMI Research Press, 1989.

Leggett, B. J. *Wallace Stevens and Poetic Theory*. Chapel Hill: University of North Carolina Press, 1987.

Lehman, David. *The Last Avant-Garde: The Making of the New York School of Poets*, New York: Doubleday, 1998.

Leibowitz, Herbert A. "A Pan Piping on the City Streets: *The Collected Poems of Frank O'Hara*." In *Frank O'Hara: To Be True to a City*, ed. Scott Elledge, 24. Ann Arbor: University of Michigan Press, 1990.

Leja, Michael. "Jackson Pollock: Representing the Unconscious." In *Reading American Art*, ed. Marianna Doezema and Elizabeth Milroy, 440–64. New Haven, CT: Yale University Press, 1998.

LeSueur, Joseph. *Digressions on Some Poems by Frank O'Hara: A Memoir*. New York: Farrar, Straus and Giroux, 2003.

Levinson, Jerrold. *The Pleasures of Aesthetics: Philosophical Essays*. Ithaca, NY: Cornell University Press, 1996.

Libby, Anthony. "O'Hara on the Silver Range." *Contemporary Literature* 17, no. 4 (1976): 14–62.

Lisk, Thomas. "An Ashbery Primer." In *The Scene of My Selves: New York on New York School Poets*, ed. Terence Diggory and Stephen Paul Miller, 35–49. Orono, ME: National Poetry Foundation, 2001.

Livingstone, Angela. Introduction to *Pasternak on Art and Creativity*. Ed. Angela Livingstone. Cambridge: Cambridge University Press, 1985.

———, ed. *Pasternak on Art and Creativity*. Cambridge: Cambridge University Press, 1985.

Longenbach, John. *Modern Poetry after Modernism*. Oxford: Oxford University Press, 1997.

———. *Stone Cottage: Pound, Yeats and Modernism.* Oxford: Oxford University Press, 1998.

Lotman, Yuri. *The Structure of the Artistic Text.* Trans. Ronald Vroon. Ann Arbor: University of Michigan Press, 1977.

Lowe, Victor. *Understanding Whitehead.* Baltimore: Johns Hopkins University Press, 1962.

Lowell, Robert. *Collected Poems.* Ed. Frank Bidart and David Gewanter. New York: Farrar, Straus and Giroux, 2003.

———. *Life Studies.* London: Faber and Faber, 1959.

Lowney, John. *The American Avant-Garde Tradition: William Carlos Williams, Postmodern Poetry, and the Politics of Cultural Memory.* Lewisburg: Bucknell University Press, 1997.

———. "The 'Post-Anti-Esthetic' Poetics of Frank O'Hara." *Contemporary Literature* 32, no. 2 (1991): 244–64.

Machacek, Gregory. "Allusion." *PMLA* 122, no. 2 (March 2007): 522–36.

Machado, Antonio. *The Selected Poems of Antonio Machado.* Trans. Betty Jean Craige. Baton Rouge: Louisiana State University Press, 1978.

MacLeod, Glen G. *Wallace Stevens and Modern Art.* New Haven, CT: Yale University Press, 1993.

Magee, Michael. "Tribes of New York: Frank O'Hara, Amiri Baraka, and the Poetics of the Five Spot." *Contemporary Literature* 42, no. 4 (Winter 2001): 694–726.

Magnus, Bernd, and Kathleen M. Higgens. "Nietzsche's Works and Their Themes." In *The Cambridge Companion to Nietzsche*, ed. Bernd Magnus and Kathleen M. Higgens, 21–68. Cambridge: Cambridge University Press, 1996.

Mallarmé, Stéphane. "Crisis in Poetry." In *Mallarmé: Selected Prose Poems, Essays, and Letters*, ed. and trans. Bardford Cook, 24–43. Baltimore: Johns Hopkins University Press, 1956.

Mason, Eudo C. *Rilke.* London: Oliver and Boyd, 1963.

Mattix, Micah. "Periodization and Difference." *New Literary History* 35, no. 4 (2004): 685–97.

Mayakovsky, Vladimir. *Love Is the Heart of Everything: Correspondence between Vladimir Mayakovsky and Lili Brik, 1915–1930.* Trans. Julian Graffy. Ed. Bengt Jangfeldt. New York: Grove Press, 1986.

———. *Mayakovsky.* Ed. Herbert Marshall, New York: Hill and Wang, 1965.

———. *Poems.* Trans. Dorian Rottenberg. Moscow: Progress, 1976.

McCarthy, Mary. "A Prince of Shreds and Patches." In *Focus on Shakespearean Films*, ed. Charles W. Eckert, 63–67. New York: Prentice Hall, 1972.

McFarland, Thomas. *Coleridge and the Pantheistic Tradition.* Oxford: Clarendon, 1969.

Meyer, Michel. "Le plaisir comme refoulement: Pour une autre psychoanalyse du corps." *Revue internationale de philosophie* 18 (2000): 481–90.

Mills, Ralph J., Jr. *Cry of the Human: Essays on Contemporary American Poetry.* Urbana: University of Illinois Press, 1975.

Milton, John. *The Complete Poems.* Ed. John Leonard. New York: Penguin, 1998.

Molesworth, Charles. "'The Clear Architecture of the Nerves': The Poetry of Frank O'Hara." *Iowa Review* 6, no. 2 (1975): 61–73.

Moramarco, Fred. "John Ashbery and Frank O'Hara: The Painterly Poets." *Journal of Modern Literature* 5, no. 3 (1976): 436–62.

Moréas, Jean. "Le symbolisme." *Figaro*, September 18, 1898, 150.

Motherwell, Robert. *The Collected Writings of Robert Motherwell.* Ed. Stephanie Terenzio. Oxford: Oxford University Press, 1992.

———. "The Modern Painter's World." In *The Writings of Robert Motherwell*, ed. Dore Ashton, 27–35. Berkeley and Los Angeles: University of California Press, 2007.

Mottram, Eric. "Frank O'Hara." In *American Poetry: The Modernist Ideal*, ed. Clive Bloom and Brian Docherty, 143–66. New York: St. Martin's, 1995.

Mure, G. R. G. *The Philosophy of Hegel.* London: Oxford University Press, 1965.

Nadeau, Maurice. *Histoire du surréalisme.* 2nd ed. Paris: Seuil, 1946.

Naso, Publius Ovidus. *Metamorphoses.* Trans. Mary M. Innes. London: Penguin, 1955.

Nichols, Ashton. *The Revolutionary "I": Wordsworth and the Politics of Self-Presentation.* London: Macmillan, 1998.

Nietzsche, Frederick. *Beyond Good and Evil: Prelude to a Philosophy of the Future.* Trans. Helen Zimmern. Vol. 12 of *The Complete Works of Frederick Nietzsche*, ed. Oscar Levey. New York: Russell and Russell, 1964.

———. *The Birth of Tragedy; or, Hellenism and Pessimism.* Trans. William A. Haussman. Vol. 1 of *The Complete Works of Frederick Nietzsche*, ed. Oscar Levy. New York: Russell and Russell, 1964.

———. *The Dawn of Day.* Trans. J. M. Kennedy. Vol. 9. *The Complete Works of Frederick Nietzsche*, ed. Oscar Levy. New York: Russell and Russell, 1964,

———. *The Twilight of the Idols; or, How to Philosophise with the Hammer.* Trans. Anthony M. Ludovic. Vol. 16. *The Complete Works of Frederick Nietzsche*, ed. Oscar Levey. New York: Russell and Russell, 1964.

Olson, Charles. *The Collected Poems of Charles Olson.* Ed. George F. Butterick. Berkeley and Los Angeles: University of California Press, 1987.

———. *Collected Prose.* Ed. Donald Allen and Benjamin Friedlander. Berkeley: University of California Press, 1997.

———. *The Maximus Poems.* Ed. George F. Butterick. Berkeley: University of California Press, 1995.

Padgett, Ron. "Four French Poets and the Cubist Painters." In *The Straight Line: Writings on Poetry and Poets*, 33–43. Ann Arbor: University of Michigan Press, 2000.

———. *Great Balls of Fire.* Minneapolis: Coffee House Press, 1990.

———. "On *The Sonnets.*" In *Nice to See You: Homage to Ted Berrigan*, ed. Anne Waldman, 9–11. Minneapolis: Coffee House Press, 1991.

Parker, Alice C. *The Exploration of the Secret Smile: The Language of Art and of Homosexuality in Frank O'Hara's Poetry.* New York: Peter Lang, 1989.

Pasternak, Boris Leonidovic. "Chopin." In *Pasternak on Art and Creativity*, ed. Angela Livingstone, 183–86. Cambridge: Cambridge University Press, 1985.

———. *Doctor Zhivago.* Trans. Max Hayward, Manya Harari, and Bernard Gilbert Guerney. New York: Pantheon, 1958.

———. "Early Prose Fragments." In *Pasternak on Art and Creativity*, ed. Angela Livingstone, 32–40. Cambridge, Cambridge University Press, 1985.

———. *My Sister-Life.* Trans. Mark Rudman with Bohdan Boychuk. Toronto: Exile, 1989.

———. "Paul-Marie Verlaine." In *Pasternak on Art and Creativity*, ed. Angela Livingstone, 179–82. Cambridge, Cambridge University Press, 1985.

———. *Safe Conduct: An Early Autobiography, and Other Works.* Trans. Beatrice Scott. New York: New Directions, 1958.

———. "Some Propositions." In *Pasternak on Art and Creativity*, ed. Angela Livingstone, 28–31. Cambridge: Cambridge University Press, 1985.

Perelman, Bob. *The Marginalization of Poetry: Language Writing and Literary History.* Princeton, NJ: Princeton University Press, 1996.

Perkins, David. *A History of Modern Poetry.* 2 vols. Cambridge, MA: Harvard University Press, 1976, 1987.

Perloff, Marjorie. *The Dance of the Intellect: Studies of Poetry in the Pound Tradition.* Cambridge: Cambridge University Press, 1985.

———. *Frank O'Hara: Poet among Painters.* 2nd ed. Chicago: University of Chicago Press, 1998.

———. "Language Poetry and the Lyric Subject: Ron Silliman's Albany, Susan Howe's Buffalo." *Critical Inquiry* 25, no. 3 (1999): 405–34.

———. "New Thresholds, Old Anatomies: Contemporary Poetry and the Limits of Exegesis." *Iowa Review* 5, no. 1 (1974): 83–89

———.*The Poetics of Indeterminacy: Rimbaud to Cage.* Princeton, NJ: Princeton University Press, 1981.

Pia, Pascal. *Baudelaire.* Paris: Seuil, 1952.

Picasso, Pablo. *Picasso in His Words.* Ed. Hiro Clark. San Francisco: Collins Publishers, 1993.

———. *Picasso on Art: A Selection of Views.* Ed. Dore Ashton. New York: Da Capo Press, 1972.

Pollock, Jackson. *Interviews, Articles, and Reviews.* Ed. Pepe Karmel and Harry N. Abrams. New York: Museum of Modern Art, 1999.

Pound, Ezra. *The Cantos of Ezra Pound.* 14th ed. New York: New Directions, 1998.

———. *Literary Essays of Ezra Pound.* Ed. T. S. Eliot. New York: New Directions, 1954.

———. *Make It New.* London: Faber and Faber, 1934.

———. *Pound's Cavalcanti.* Ed. David Anderson. Princeton, NJ: Princeton University Press, 1983.

———. *Selected Poems.* Ed. T. S. Eliot. London: Faber and Faber, 1949.

Quinney, Laura. *The Poetics of Disappointment: Wordsworth to Ashbery.* Charlottesville: University Press of Virginia, 1999.

Raymond, Marcel. *De Baudelaire au surréalisme.* Paris: José Corti, 1966.

Reed, Brian M. "Twentieth-Century Poetry and the New York Art World." In *A Concise Companion to Twentieth-Century American Poetry*, ed. Stephen Fredman, 113–34. London: Blackwell, 2005.

Rehder, Robert. *The Poetry of Wallace Stevens.* London: Macmillan, 1988.

———. *Wordsworth and the Beginnings of Modern Poetry.* Totowa, NJ: Barnes and Noble, 1981.

Reverdy, Pierre. *Selected Poems.* Trans. John Ashbery, Mary Ann Caws, and Patricia Terry. Ed. Timothy Bent. Winston Salem, NC: Wake Forest University Press, 1991.

Richardson, Dorothy. "Saintsbury and Art for Art's Sake in England." *PMLA* 59, no. 1 (1944): 243–60.

Rifkin, Libbie. " 'Worrying about Making It': Ted Berrigan's Social Poetics." *Contemporary Literature* 38, no. 4 (2008): 640–72.

Rilke, Rainer Maria. *Duino Elegies and The Sonnets to Orpheus.* Trans. A. Poulin Jr. Boston: Houghton Mifflin Company, 1977.

———. *Letters to a Young Poet.* Trans. M. D. Herter Norton. New York: W. W. Norton, 1934.

———. *New Poems.* Trans. Edward Snow. New York: North Point Press, 2001.

Rimbaud, Arthur. *Œuvres complètes.* Ed. Antoine Adam. Paris: Gallimard, 1972.

Rivers, Larry. "Life among the Stones." *Location,* Spring 1963, 93–97.

———. *What Did I Do? An Unauthorized Autobiography.* With Arnold Weinstein. New York: Aaron Asher Books, 1992.

Robbe-Grillet, Alain. *For a New Novel: Essays on Fiction.* Trans. Richard Howard. New York: Grove Press, 1965.

Rosenberg, Harold. "The American Action Painters." *ArtNews* 51, no. 8 (December 1952): 22–23, 48–50.

Ross, Andrew. *The Failure of Modernism: Symptoms of American Poetry.* New York: Columbia University Press, 1986.

Roth, Charles Smith. *Understanding Alain Robbe-Grillet.* Columbia: University of South Carolina Press, 2000.

Ruland, Richard, and Malcom Bradbury. *From Puritanism to Postmodernism: A History of American Literature.* London: Routledge, 1991.

Rzepka, Charles J. *The Self as Mind: Vision and Identity in Wordsworth, Coleridge, and Keats.* Cambridge, MA: Harvard University Press, 1986.

Saussure, Ferdinand de. *Cours de linguistique générale.* Ed. Charles Bailly and Albert Séchehaye, with assistance from Albert Riedlinger. Paris: Payot, 1995.

Schmidt, Peter. "The Improvisations: Williams, Dada, and the Theory of Automatic Writing." In *William Carlos Williams, the Arts, and Literary Tradition,* 90–135. Baton Rouge: Louisiana State University Press, 1988.

Schwartz, Delmore. *In Dreams Begin Responsibilities.* New York: New Directions, 1978.

Selerie, Gavin. "Charles Olson." In *American Poetry: The Modernist Ideal,* ed. Clive Bloom and Brian Docherty, 167–98. New York: St. Martin's, 1995.

Shapiro, David. "Art as Collaboration: Toward a Theory of Pluralist Aesthetics, 1950–1980." In *Artistic Collaboration in the Twentieth Century,* ed. Cynthia Jaffee McCabe, 50–53. Washington, DC: Smithsonian Institution Press, 1984.

———. *New and Selected Poems* (1965–2006). New York: Overlook Press, 2007.

Shaw, Lytle. *Frank O'Hara: The Poetics of Coterie.* Iowa City: University of Iowa Press, 2006.

Sheehan, Peter J. "Crane's 'Moment Fugue.'" *The Explicator* 31 (1978): 151–52.

Shklovsky, Victor. "Art as Technique." In *Modern Literary Theory,* ed. Philip Rice and Patricia Waugh, 17–22. London: Arnold, 1989.

Shoptaw, John. *On the Outside Looking Out: John Ashbery's Poetry*. Cambridge, MA: Harvard University Press, 1994.

Silliman, Ron, et al. "Aesthetic Tendency and the Politics of Poetry: A Manifesto." *Social Text* 19/20 (1988): 261–75.

———. "Who Speaks: Ventriloquism and the Self in the Poetry Reading." In *Close Listening: Poetry and the Performed Word*, ed. Charles Bernstein, 360–78. Oxford: Oxford University Press, 1988.

Simms, Eva-Maria. "Uncanny Dolls: Images of Death in Rilke and Freud." *New Literary History* 27, no. 4 (Autumn 1996): 663–77.

Smith, Hazel. *Hyperscapes in the Poetry of Frank O'Hara: Difference, Homosexuality, Topography*. Liverpool: Liverpool University Press, 2000.

Sorrentino, Gilbert. "The New Note." In *Frank O'Hara: To Be True to a City*, ed. Scott Elledge, 15. Ann Arbor: University of Michigan Press, 1990.

Spies, Werner. "An Open-Ended Oeuvre." Trans. John Gabriel. In *Max Ernst: Dada and the Dawn of Surrealism*, ed. Simon Haviland, 17–30. Munich: Prestel Verlag and the Menil Collection, 1993.

Stein, Gertrude. *Tender Buttons*. Los Angeles: Sun and Moon Press, 1990.

Stein, Kevin. "'Everything the Opposite' of History: A Literary Basis for the Anti-Literary in Frank O'Hara's Lunch Poems." In *Private Poets, Worldly Acts: Public and Private History in Contemporary American Poetry*, 43–46. Athens: Ohio University Press, 1996.

Stevens, Wallace. *The Collected Poems of Wallace Stevens*. New York: Vintage, 1990.

———. *The Necessary Angel: Essays on Reality and the Imagination*. New York: Knopf, 1951.

———. *Opus Posthumous*. London: Faber and Faber, 1989.

Strong, Beret E. *The Poetic Avant-Garde: The Groups of Borges, Auden and Breton*. Evanston, IL: Northwestern University Press, 1997.

Sussman, Henry. "Prolegomena to Any Present and Future Language Poetry." *Modern Language Notes (MLN)* 118, no. 5 (2003): 1193–1212.

Sweet, David LeHardy. *Savage Sight, Constructed Noise: Poetic Adaptations of Painterly Techniques in the French and American Avant-Gardes*. Chapel Hill: University of North Carolina Press, 2003.

Tashjian, Dicktran. *A Boatload of Madmen: Surrealism and the American Avant-Garde, 1920–1950*. London: Thames and Hudson, 1995.

Tate, James. *The Lost Pilot*. New Haven, CT: Yale University Press, 1967.

———. *Oblivion Ha-Ha*. Boston: Little, Brown and Co., 1970.

———. *Viper Jazz*. Middletown, CT: Wesleyan University Press, 1972.

Tennyson, Alfred, Lord. *In Memoriam*. Ed. Susan Shatto and Marion Shaw. Oxford: Clarendon Press, 1982.

Todorov, Tzvetan. "Une complication de texte: Les *Illuminations*." *Poétique* 34 (1978): 241–53.

Trilling, Lionel. *Sincerity and Authenticity*. London: Oxford University Press, 1972.

Tsvetaeva, Marina. "Art in the Light of Conscience." In *Modern Russian Poets on Poetry*, ed. Carl R. Proffer, trans. Angela Livingstone and V. S. Coe, 145–84. Ann Arbor, MI: Ardis, 1976.

Valéry, Paul. *Œuvres*. Ed. Jean Hytier. 2 vols. Paris: Pléiade, 1957–60.

Vendler, Helen. *Part of Nature, Part of Us*. Cambridge, MA: Harvard University Press, 1980.

Waldman, Anne. *Fast Speaking Woman: Chants and Essays*. San Francisco: City Lights Books, 1975.

———. ed. *Nice to See You: Homage to Ted Berrigan*. Minneapolis: Coffee House Press, 1991.

———, ed. *Out of this World: An Anthology of the St. Mark's Poetry Project, 1966–1991*. New York: Crown Publishers, 1991.

Waldrop, Keith. *The Locality Principle*. Berkeley, CA: Avec Books, 1995.

Ward, Geoff. *Statutes of Liberty: The New York School of Poets*. London: Palgrave, 2001.

Waswo, Richard. "The 'Autonomy of Art' Is a Wish, Not a Fact." *Criticism* 22, no. 4 (Fall 1980): 341–56.

Watson, Dana Cairns. *Gertrude Stein and the Essence of What Happens*. Nashville, TN: Vanderbilt University Press, 2005.

Weaver, Mike. *William Carlos Williams: The American Background*. Cambridge: Cambridge University Press, 1971.

Wechsler, Jeffrey. *Surrealism and American Art, 1931–1947*. New Brunswick, NJ: Rutgers University Art Gallery, 1976.

Wendell, Barrett. "Walt Whitman." In *Leaves of Grass*, ed. Sculley Bradley and Harold W. Blodgett, 813–20. New York: W. W. Norton, 1973.

Whitehead, Alfred North. *Modes of Thought*. New York: Free Press, 1966.

———. *Process and Reality*. New York: Free Press, 1957.

Whitman, Walt. *Leaves of Grass*. Ed. Sculley Bradley and Harold Blodgett. New York: New York University Press, 1965.

———. *Notebooks and Unpublished Prose Manuscripts*. Ed. Edward F. Grier. 6 vols. New York: New York University Press, 1984.

Williams, William Carlos. *The Collected Poems of William Carlos Williams*. Ed. Christopher MacGowan. 2 vols. New York: New Directions, 1991.

———. *Imaginations*. Ed. Webster Scott. New York: New Directions, 1970.

———. *In the American Grain*. Norfolk, CT: New Directions, 1956.

———. *Paterson*. 5 vols. New York: New Directions, 1946–58.

———. "Prologue to *Kora in Hell*." In *Selected Essays of William Carlos Williams*, 3–26. New York: Random House, 1954.

Williamson, Alan. "Diffracting Diamond: Ashbery, Romanticism, and Anti-Art." In *Introspection and Contemporary Poetry*, 116–48. Cambridge, MA: Harvard University Press, 1984.

Winnicott, D. W. *Playing and Reality*. New York: Basic, 1971.

Wohl, Hellmut. *The Aesthetics of Italian Renaissance Art: A Reconsideration of Style*. Cambridge: Cambridge University Press, 1999.

Woods, Tim. *The Poetics of the Limit: Ethics and Politics in Modern and Contemporary American Poetry*. London: Palgrave Macmillan, 2002.

Wordsworth, William. *Lyrical Ballads*. Ed. Michael Mason. London: Longman, 1992.

———. *The Prelude*. Ed. W. J. B. Owen. Ithaca, NY: Cornell University Press, 1985.

Yeats, W. B. *The Autobiography of William Butler Yeats: Consisting of "Reveries over Childhood and Youth," "The Trembling of the Veil," and "Dramatis Personae."* 2nd ed. New York: Macmillan, 1953.

———. *The Collected Poems of W. B. Yeats.* Ed. Richard J. Finneran. 2nd ed. New York: Scribner, 1996.

Yenser, Stephen. *Circle to Circle: The Poetry of Robert Lowell.* Berkeley and Los Angeles: University of California Press, 1975.

Audiovisual Materials

Baraka, Amiri. *Amiri Baraka.* film VHS. Poetry Center and San Francisco State University, San Francisco, March 2, 1977.

Index